HOW TO
GET WHAT
YOU **WANT**
IN 7 WEEKS

THE JOURNEY TO
RE-DISCOVERING YOUR
AUTHENTIC SELF

Julie Provino

RETHINK PRESS

First published in Great Britain 2018
by Rethink Press (www.rethinkpress.com)

To my loving family,
Jude and Celeste:
you are my world.

CONTENTS

INTRODUCTION

The purpose of this book is to help people achieve self-actualisation and live a fuller and more meaningful life, thriving and achieving success. My wish is not to sell a solution to fix everything, but to share with you some of my experiences of personal transformation, giving you the opportunity to find yourself.

Sometimes life throws us a curve ball and we all need a bit of help. In this book, I will introduce you to a different concept each week: an idea to work on and exercises to help you establish what you want, then go out and get it. I've used simple ideas and real examples[1] to share the learning that has enabled me to live the extraordinarily rich life that I do today.

It wasn't always like this. I grew up in what I would call normal circumstances, with great parents trying to do their best despite a messy divorce. I had good friends, good family, good academic achievements, etc.

And then came trauma – one of those times when your life seems to crumble from under your feet, you lose all sense of direction, and the future is a big mess. When I was fifteen, on top of going through the normal teenage angst, I experienced a car crash that took me years to

---

1   The names in this book are fictitious, to protect people's privacy.

recover from. I wasn't a 'survivor'; I just had to get on with it. The physical damage caused by the accident obviously took time to heal, but the mental impact was even greater.

It was only in my late twenties, after years of psychiatric support, that I discovered I was suffering from post-traumatic stress disorder (PTSD) – a condition in which your emotions become bigger than you and rather uncontrollable. It was a pretty lonely place to be back then.

The therapists I was seeing focused on my past, asking, 'Tell me, how do you feel about that?' rather than empowering me to move forward. I often left the therapy room in tears despite feedback that it had been a good session. I had the perfect Facebook life: many friends, good academic achievements, great relationship with my partner, and a promising career ahead of me. But I felt completely hollow.

I began to study various disciplines, and my curiosity about how people do what they do increased. I became a pretty good human resources leader, developing great people reading skills and knowledge of international employment law and practices to the point where I set up my own consultancy back in 2013. I'm also a trainer and coach, delivering tangible results and high satisfaction to all of my clients. Sharing my passion for what I do is what makes me tick, so it became my mission to be a beacon of hope to many out there who still think that life should be about the 9–5.

I was curious about neurolinguistic programming (NLP), and once I began exploring this concept, it swallowed me whole. My trainer helped me to realise that I am at the cause side of the cause and effect equation. How I manage my own emotion and behaviour is something that I can work with rather than battle against. I became an avid fan of observing and modelling others and myself, unleashing tremendous potential. I am now an NLP trainer, mindfulness coach, HR guru, motivational speaker and blogger, among many things and I'm constantly expanding my knowledge.

The world is going through changes and people are waking up to the fact that they can have control over their destinies. They can break moulds in their personal and professional lives, and I enjoy watching this process take place. I hope that this book will help everyone achieve what they want. It can be easy and fun to work on who you are and reap the benefits of your hard work.

This book is comprised of seven chapters, each representing a week (or longer if you need it) of your journey, and it is accompanied by a workbook that can be ordered from www.verytraining.co.uk, my training company. Most importantly enjoy the process and discover more about yourself. Break out of the moulds – we are all human, and we are all unique.

Week One

So Tell Me, What Do You Want?

This book is not solely about getting what you want; it is about knowing what you want, being fully attuned to who you are and where you are going. When you are so congruent within yourself that nothing stops you getting what you want, life gets easier and more enjoyable.

We will follow my journey of discovery while guiding you through your story and experiences. Take it as quickly or slowly as you like; I would just encourage you to use your time and energy well and focus your attention on being authentic with yourself to achieve maximum results.

What is it that you want?

When I was a young girl I was often asked, 'What do you want to be when you grow up?' For most children, the response is usually 'A fireman', 'A teacher', 'A vet', or something equally definite. Yet as time flies by, the answer becomes trickier. With an increasing number of deadlines, commitments, dramas and responsibilities, it becomes more challenging to know what you are, and sometimes even who you are.

Several years back, I thought I had it all sussed: married mother with a successful career. What else could a woman in her early thirties want? I had it all. Then something happened. It felt like I had woken up properly for the first time ever. I was able to see my life for what it actually was: the envy of many strangers, but completely empty of meaning. My friends didn't know me, and I didn't know myself. I couldn't even say what my favourite meal was any more. Life had become bland and tasteless.

I looked at the decisions I had made over the last thirty years that had led me to who I was back then and realised I had come to the end of that particular cycle, but I didn't know how to move forward.

Speaking to friends and family about my predicament, I was often asked, 'Well, what do you want?' That was easy. I wanted to be happy. That said, I couldn't define what happiness was for me specifically at that time.

Now don't get me wrong, I know exactly how to feel happy. I can think of a beautiful memory and recall the feelings of happiness. But being happy in the long term is more of an art than a science. To achieve such a goal, you need to know what it is that you want.

In the first week of your journey, we will start by observing all the different facets of you. Layer by layer, we will discover the change that you are looking for and then work on achieving that change. Treat this as a journey of self-discovery, curiosity and fun.

Right now, I would like to shake your hand and congratulate you. You have achieved your first step by purchasing this book. The next one is as easy as this one, and so is the next one, and the next...

Now is exactly the right time for you to begin your journey. You may currently be feeling a sense of unease, but unease is just a symptom of change. Change can be exciting or difficult; it all depends how you have framed it in your mind. This book, and maybe even the accompanying workbook, will be your companion and enable you to think positively about change and make it long lasting.

At this stage, we are looking for the big picture (we'll go into the detail later). Life is short, yet many people don't find the time to do the things they really want to do. Usually this is because they either think it can wait, or are scared. Consider how you want your life to be. Who are you, and what do you want to be recognised for?

Imagine you have decided to take part in a marathon. You will need to plan your nutrition, training, footwear, and get into the right headspace to make sure you get the best possible outcome. Using the analogy to represent your journey towards change, I would recommend that you start your planning activity right now.

The Four Stages of Learning model

I want to share with you the Four Stages of Learning model which will help you to understand the underpinning principles behind this book. The model demonstrates the stages we go through while learning. There will be moments of doubt, frustration, joy and achievement, and it is good to acknowledge this now. We do not become marathon runners as soon as we put our running shoes on for the first time. It will take dedication, practice and focus.

To illustrate the model, we will use the example of learning to drive a car.

First stage: unconscious incompetence. A three-year-old child does not know that she cannot drive a car, and she probably doesn't care. She is unconscious about her incompetence.

Generally speaking, individuals are not too bothered at this stage as they do not recognise the value of learning a skill. When they start to realise the benefit of a new skill, they move to the next stage.

Second stage: conscious incompetence. At some point in time, the child will realise that she is not able to drive. She may say that in a few years, she will learn to drive. She is conscious about her incompetence.

People want to learn something once they have found out how it could benefit them. This is where awareness comes in. In my training and coaching practice, we constantly work on the awareness factor, as this is where true change begins and we start doing core foundational work, which is the transition to the next stage.

Third stage: conscious competence. When the girl reaches seventeen, she can learn to drive in the UK. Taking her time and practising the individual skills, she will gradually become a competent driver. She will be conscious that she can now drive a car (her new competency), but to begin with she will do it with extra care.

Moving from stage two to stage three can be uncomfortable as we are in the training and practice stage. This means we will make mistakes or fail at times – for example, a learner driver will often stall the car. With persistence and motivation, which come from believing the skill will benefit us, we move to the next stage.

Fourth stage: unconscious competence. After some years, the girl will drive from A to B without thinking too much about indicating or changing lanes. She will do these things naturally as she has refined her skill over time.

This is when a new skill becomes second nature, and we are often able to do other things alongside it.

Focus

Focus on what you want, then set your brain and your energy to get it. This works with your unconscious mind.

I have studied the unconscious (sometimes called the subconscious) mind for several years, and it is clear to me that all learning, all change, all habits take place at this level. When we tell ourselves what to do or not to do consciously, it wastes a lot of energy and seldom helps us to be successful in what we are seeking to achieve.

Early research demonstrated that our mind is only able to focus on seven things simultaneously. But in April 2014, *Proceedings of the National Academy of Sciences* reduced that number to three or four things. To achieve exactly what you want successfully, you need to be focused on that one thing. If you want to change career, find true love, lose weight, stop biting your nails, generate a new income, and find a new hobby, the likelihood of you achieving all of that in seven weeks is slim, so focus on one thing at a time and set yourself achievable goals and milestones. Then let the new habits become integrated into your being.

If you want someone to like you, for example, focus on your actions to achieve that outcome for yourself. We cannot force people to like us; we can only be responsible for how we choose to act, think and be.

Imagine getting in your car to travel to work. You know which direction to go, but this morning things are a little different. Sometimes you turn the steering wheel and the car responds, other times it does not. Sometimes you apply the brakes and the car slows down, at other times it does not. Sometimes the car accelerates when you push down on the accelerator, other times it does not. There is nowhere to pull over on the motorway, so for a little while you are stumped about what to do. Then you notice a blinking red light on your dashboard and realise your car is being remotely controlled. Providing you are driving in the direction the remote controller wants you to go, all is well. When you try to drive in a different direction, things don't go as planned.

> *'You've got to be very careful if you don't know where you are going, because you might not get there.'*
>
> **YOGI BERRA**

Driving a car that is remotely controlled is like living a life unknowingly controlled by your unconscious mind.

I remember talking with a woman as part of a coaching programme. Liza's issue was that she did not want children, which was causing tension in her marriage. Going deeper into her issue, we realised that her life was based on the expectations of her mother and father. They had wished for her to have a perfect family and a perfect job, but what was important for Liza was not linked to those two desires. She wanted freedom and exploration.

Liza became an inspiration to me. She took courageous steps to seek the life that she really wanted for herself, got comfortable with her own choices, ultimately getting what she wanted, not what her parents wanted for her.

Be clear on what you want. What is the purpose behind the purpose? Is it your own purpose, or that of other people? And if it is the latter, what do *you* truly want?

EXERCISE 1

Sit in a peaceful environment where you know you won't be interrupted for at least fifteen minutes. Take a pen and paper with you.

Breathe deeply into your abdomen while thinking about what you want. What will that look like when you have achieved it? Continue to relax, thinking positive thoughts that move you forward on your journey.

Once you are clear on where your journey is taking you, think about what you want again. What do you want to achieve today? What is the purpose behind that? Listen to the first thought you have, and be honest with yourself. Write down whatever comes to mind even if it doesn't make much sense right now.

Now ask yourself, 'Is there another purpose behind that?' If there is, write it down. Continue this exercise until nothing else comes up.

Before resuming your day-to-day activities, thank yourself for being honest. Are your goals clear to you? Have they changed? Keep those questions open for the rest of the day.

Understanding your mind – the scientific bit

To understand how our unconscious mind has such incredible power, we are going to look at our brain – what it does and how it works.

The brain is a connection machine; its function is to associate, connect and link information. Thoughts, memories, skills and attributes are vast sets of connections joined together via complex chemical and physical pathways. Each person's brain is different to anyone else's, and this is what makes us perfect.

The brain has around 100 billion neurons. Each neuron has up to 100,000 dendrites gathering information for the neurons, and one axon which passes on the information the dendrites have collected. The number of possible ways in which neurons in the brain could be connected is larger than the number of known atoms in the universe.

When you hear a new idea, you create a picture or a map of that idea in your mind, then compare it to your existing maps. The connections between your neurons are the maps that guide your thoughts, behaviours and actions.

As there is an almost unlimited number of ways in which experiences, learning and information can be coded in the brain, no two people think in the same way, have the same perspective on a situation, feel the same or believe exactly the same things. People hear even the simplest things differently.

Our brain can only hold three or four ideas in working memory at any one time. As we are constantly bombarded by a vast amount of information, our brain likes to hardwire any actions that we do repeatedly so they do not take up limited working memory space, which is how we generate habits. For example, elite athletes have hardwired many sport skills that the rest of us struggle to master. Adults have hardwired the ability to walk and do it unconsciously, while toddlers still concentrate on walking. When it hardwires something, the brain pushes the map it has created down into the subcortex which holds long-term memories and processes, and has a far greater capacity than working memory.

Your hardwiring drives your perception. Since the time of ancient Greece, philosophers and scholars have concluded that we see the world as we are, not as the world is. In a sense, we create our own reality. We are the cause of everything we do.

> *'Let him that would move
> the world first move himself.'*
>
> ───────────
>
> **SOCRATES**

> *'The world we see that seems so insane
> is the result of a belief system that is not
> working. To perceive the world differently,
> we must be willing to change our
> belief system, let the past slip away,
> expand our sense of now, and dissolve
> the fear in our mind.'*
>
> ───────────
>
> **WILLIAM JAMES**

When we hear something new, we compare it to our existing internal maps to see where the connections are. Our brain will do everything it can to make the new information fit into our existing maps.

For example, when we are in favour of an idea, we are more likely to accept the most tenuous evidence confirming its validity as fact. When we are not in favour of an idea, we will see even strong evidence confirming its validity as irrelevant. I believe that it is important to push the boundaries of our thinking to dissolve the fear in our mind. Anything is possible; anything that we set our mind to can happen.

This is where curiosity will get you a long way.

Your unconscious

Our lives can be a lot like attempting to drive the remotely controlled vehicle we mentioned earlier. The driver is your conscious mind and the remote controller is your unconscious mind. When they both agree on the direction, driving is easy. When they disagree, it is virtually impossible to drive the vehicle in a different direction from that chosen by the remote controller. But while it may be difficult to drive a car that is being remotely controlled by someone else, it is possible to take over the role of remote controller in your life.

Your unconscious performs two very important tasks for you: filtering information and running strategies. It can perform these tasks in a way that empowers you (and assists you to drive in the direction you seek) or disempowers you (and hinders you from driving in the direction you seek).

It is difficult to change your unconscious mind until you become aware of what it is doing. One of the best ways to become aware is to pay close attention to how you behave in different situations and notice the things you do automatically. These are the clues to how your unconscious is operating. And this is exactly what mindfulness is about.

> *[Mindfulness is] 'a mental state achieved by focusing one's awareness on the present moment, while calmly acknowledging and accepting one's feelings, thoughts, and bodily sensations. Used as a therapeutic technique.'*
> **WIKIPEDIA**

As a human being, we are subjected to over 2 million bits of information per second via our five senses of sight, hearing, touch, smell and taste. Our brain, according to its standard anatomy, can process up to 124 bits per second. To protect us from mental overwhelm, a part of our brain known as the Reticular Activating System (RAS) chooses which bits of information go into our conscious mind and which go into our unconscious mind through a process called filtering.

The RAS consistently filters information in the same way until either we choose to change it or an event happens of such magnitude that we are forced to change it. As we all like to be right, our RAS filters information to confirm existing long-held beliefs and disregards information which would be contrary to those beliefs.

We choose our current unconscious filters as a result of our upbringing, environment and significant emotional experiences. The filters include our values, beliefs, attitudes, memories, decisions and language, which combined make up our mindset. Many of the connections creating our mindset are firmly wired in our neurology. They define how we see the world, the choices we make and the results we produce without conscious awareness.

It is possible to change our unconscious connections, and the best way is to create new connections. There is a difference between a thought (a map held in our working memory) and a habit (a map that's hardwired in the deeper parts of our brain), but it's not difficult to bridge the gap between the two.

If we want to hardwire a new behaviour, we need to give our mental map enough attention over time to ensure it becomes embedded in our brain. We do this by making links to different parts of the brain so that the web of links thickens and spreads out. Instead of thinking about a new idea, we write it down, speak about it and take action. By writing up our goals and journaling regularly, we can focus our thoughts and our unconscious on what we want, activating our RAS.

If you haven't heard of it before, I would encourage you to research neurolinguistic techniques, some of which are presented in this book. These support your efforts to make a positive difference to your hardwired thinking patterns. As a trainer of NLP, I have seen individuals making life-enhancing changes in a matter of weeks if not days. For some, it just feels like switching on their brains. Once you realise that you have choices and you own your destiny, the rest is empowerment and finding the right resources to get what you want.

Research has shown that neurons need positive feedback to create long-term connections, so make sure that either you are giving yourself positive feedback on your progress, or you have someone else to do it for you. You are the most important person in your life, so be kind to yourself. You deserve it.

As human beings, we have over 90,000 thoughts going through our heads each day. Our way of thinking is malleable, so when we focus on what we don't want, then that is exactly what happens. It's based on the principles of the Law of Attraction.

Everyone needs a sense of purpose in life. That is the reason we set goals in the first place. Regrettably, though, a lot of people leave everything to chance and make excuses: 'It's not me, it's how I was brought up'; 'It's not me, it's the system'; 'I can't do it, it's simply too difficult.' In my case, I was paralysed by the thought that I was my own worst enemy and had no control over what my mind could do. These people – and at one time I would have included myself – often believe they won't accomplish their goals, so fear forbids them from trying.

> *'A life lived in fear is a life half lived.'*
>
> ———————
>
> **SPANISH PROVERB**

Prior to setting goals for yourself, know what you want in life to activate the RAS to focus on it. This is crucially important. The opportunity to be successful exists in each and every one of us in varying degrees, but we must understand what we want in order to recognise a good opportunity when it comes our way. A careful plan of action is necessary.

Milestones

Write down everything that you want to accomplish. Go on, have fun. Be creative. Even better, write it with a friend. At this stage, it does not matter whether they're small or large goals. Just prepare a list of all the things you'd prefer to do, have or own.

Not so long ago, I was in a corporate job where I didn't feel like I was adding any value. This situation made me unhappy at home and caused me to retreat from my friends, which in turn made me lonely and bordering on depression. Was this the way my life was going to be?

I remember talking to a friend who asked me what I wanted. I replied that I wanted to add value in my work role, make a positive difference to my colleagues, and be successful.

Then my friend asked me, 'Imagine the day after you retire. What will have truly mattered to you over the years?'

None of my pain mattered. My current role didn't matter. What I really wanted was to add value beyond the realms of what I believed possible. As if I had lifted myself up from the problem and could see something bigger and more important, I started thinking of my life as a journey to a destination beyond the mundane and the struggles I was facing. The same happened several years back, when I realised that I was not my disease, that I didn't have to live in fear of what could or would happen. It dawned on me that I could choose my outcome, and that being part of the 'norm' was simply abiding by expectations that others had placed on me. The realisation that I, just like you, deserved much better than that, began with one small decision.

When you're writing your goals, think about your ultimate value. Where is your journey taking you? Where is your destination?

Once you know where you are going, reflect back on where your life is today. Sometimes, it is good to step back and think about your life in sections.

Here is a simple exercise that I would encourage you to run for yourself. It is called the Wheel of Life and can also be found on http://verytraining.co.uk/wheel. Rate your life, on a scale of 0–10 (10 being right where you want to be), on where you think you are in each of the following categories.

Diagram licensed under CC BY-SA

Once you have done this, ask yourself where you want your life to be in relation to the points in the picture in seven weeks, six months, a year and so on, and notice the difference(s). Choose no more than five goals you could achieve in each category. Some of these achievements may be things you can accomplish soon, others may take more time. List short-term achievements that can be accomplished in under seven weeks, medium-term goals that will take up to three months, and long-term achievements for five to ten years time. Set up realistic time limits to achieve your chosen goals.

Reflect on what you want to achieve for yourself. Be brief and positive. Give those neurons some encouraging feedback.

For larger goals, list the small steps that you want to take to accomplish them. Create realistic goals, but stretch yourself a little. Check that they make your heart sing. Does each goal excite you? As you attain each goal, you will acquire more confidence to go on to the next one.

Trust in yourself, stay confident and pursue your success relentlessly – no excuses. By setting meaningful goals, you are comfortably on your way to changing your life for the better. Commit now to a worthier future.

Fine-tuning your goals

Your goals may start off with good intentions, but may not remain as powerful in the long term. And we are preparing for a marathon, right?

When you want something, it puts all the focus on the fact that you don't have it. What you focus on is what will happen in your life. You are the master of your own universe, after all.

What you are focusing on is evidenced by how you speak about it. The words you say and think are a reflection of what you believe in your heart. That is why what you say and think is so important. I encourage you to journal as this is like liasing directly with your unconscious.

Let go of negative self-talk

One evening, a wise old Cherokee told his grandson about a battle that was going on inside him.

'My grandson, the battle is between two wolves. One is evil, represented by anger, envy, sorrow, regret, greed, arrogance, self-pity, guilt, resentment, inferiority, lies, false pride, and ego. The other is good, represented by joy, peace, love, hope, serenity, humility, kindness, benevolence, empathy, generosity, truth, compassion and faith.'

The grandson thought about it for a minute, and then asked, 'Which wolf wins the battle?'

The grandfather simply replied, 'The one I feed.'

Do your best to leave excuses behind. If you constantly tell yourself, 'I'm too tired/bored/scared/unhappy' or 'I'm not rich/good-looking/smart enough', you're believing in a story that's designed to keep you stuck in a rut. The great news is that the story can change as you are the one writing it. Make up a different story and shape a different set of circumstances. After my accident, I was told that it would take months for me to get full use of my legs back. Like a stubborn teenager, and with the help of an amazing physiotherapist, I decided otherwise.

I decided that I would start school with both feet on the ground, which I did. That took hard work and discipline, and it kept me going all summer – a small challenge to prove that I was alive and still had control over my body.

As soon as you have identified your goals, write them in the present tense, for example *I am successful* or *I am healthy*. Write them as if you have already achieved them and put yourself in the right mindset.

Examine what paradigms or prophecies are shaping your mood, attitude, actions and behaviours. Listen when you talk to yourself. If you want a real eye-opener, jot down the things you say under your breath or in your head. You may be shocked at the limiting, judgemental, negative, critical stuff that pours through your brain. We will work on this negative self-talk next week, so you can prepare now to let go of it and rewrite your story. Once you are aware, you have the power to change.

When I started journaling my thoughts, I was amazed at the language I used to describe myself. I used to hate my own reflection and avoided looking at it like the plague. Today, I truly believe that I am an amazing creature. Just by noticing my negative internal talk, I was able to change my thinking and make a positive difference in my life.

There are times when we unintentionally use ineffective words. Here is a small list for you to think about:

- Should, could, would – these are called model operators in NLP

- But – whatever you put before 'but' will be completely invalidated

- Try – 'try' already sets you up for potential failure

- Why – 'why' has a judgemental element to it, so use it sparingly

Reprogramming your internal chatter may not result in an immediate turnaround of your fortunes, but with a new, positive mindset, you'll start feeling much better about yourself. Others will then feel better about being around you, and it'll only be a matter of time before your external circumstances match your internal mantra.

Week one guidelines

Set your goal(s), making sure they are truly what you want, and not what someone else wants for you. I am not suggesting that you live and breathe your goals during the whole seven-week period. Instead, relax into goal mode and make them your unconscious competence. Let them flow.

Stay positively focused. This is crucial. Sometimes in our desire to achieve a goal, we become impatient, and when we don't get immediate results, we become discouraged. A seed does not develop into a tree overnight; it takes time and attention.

This is where mindfulness, meditation, getting away from the hustle and bustle of everyday life comes in.

Never reject ideas or information. Hidden deep within us is a source of innovative ideas. Musicians, authors, scientists, inventors, designers, artists, etc., successfully tap into and rely on these ideas. Often, they will pop into our mind when we least expect them. We could be at work, doing housework, on the computer, or even watching TV. That is why creative people aim to keep a pad and pencil handy at all times.

When these ideas come, do not reject them because they do not fit in with whatever you are doing. That will only cut off the flow of creativity. Sometimes, there are clues hidden within the ideas that may lead you to accomplishing your goals. As the saying goes, 'The devil is in the details'.

Note down all ideas that come to you. You can decide later which ones you want to use, eliminating or storing the rest for future reference.

Be organised. Creating an outline or a plan organises your thoughts and ideas, establishing order from chaotic insights or inspirations. Without a plan, your goals will lack direction.

EXERCISE 2

Let's set your goals in a positive, long-term and fulfilling fashion.

For this exercise, relax in your favourite space. You may want to have a candle burning or soft music playing in the background. Make sure you are not interrupted. The more relaxed you are, the more in tune with your subconscious you can be.

Write down the first answer that comes to mind when you ask yourself the following questions:

- What specifically do I want?

- Where am I now?

- What will I see, hear, feel, etc., when I have it?

Remember to describe your future goals in the present tense, as if you have already achieved them, e.g. *I am healthy.* Make this future image compelling; see yourself in the picture. If it helps, create a moodboard, or imagine the future in fine detail. Add some music – whatever works for you.

We will work further on the compelling side of our goals in Week Three.

Once you've specified your present situation and the future outcome you want, ask yourself:

- How will I know when I have it?

- Is it fully desirable?

- What will this outcome allow me to do?

- Is it self-initiated and self-maintained? Is it only for me?

- Is it appropriately contextualised – where, when, how, and with whom do I want it?

- What do I have now, and what do I need to get my outcome?

- Have I ever had or done this before?

- Do I know anyone else who has?

- Can I act as if I have it?

- Is it good and positive for me, and family and friends around me?

- Is it good for the community overall?

- Why do I want this?

- What will I gain or lose if I have it?

When you visualise your goals, be sure that the projection touches all five senses. For example, if you're thinking about owning a house by the seaside, clearly see the picture of your ideal house, hear the voices of your kids playing on the sand, taste the flavour of the freshly made mojito that you are drinking, feel the warm breeze gently blowing over your face and under your T-shirt, and smell the sea air.

> 'People are not lazy. They simply
> have impotent goals – that is, goals
> that do not inspire them.'
>
> ———————
>
> **TONY ROBBINS**

When you're going through the list of your goals, they should put a feeling of exhilaration in your heart and a wide smile on your face. Every time you imagine yourself attaining these goals, you feel more powerful and joyful.

The choices we make shape our outcome, so be conscious of every choice you make every day. Think about where you will be in a year, two years, or even five years. What do you need to achieve within the next week, seven weeks, six months to get there?

Determination

Setting goals is one thing, achieving them is quite another.

> *'Goals in writing are dreams with deadlines.'*
>
> ———
>
> **BRIAN TRACY**

I have been an on/off dieter for many decades now, which has contributed to me putting on more and more weight. When I'm looking at the goal of losing weight, I am 100% determined to achieve it. I write *I will lose 0.5kg per week, I will be 10kg lighter by September* or *I will comfortably fit into that dress by Christmas*, and for a short while, I'm on course. I focus on my eating and exercising, and I have all the knowledge I need to lose weight.

Interestingly, as soon as I lose a bit of weight, feel better about myself, and enjoy the positive feedback from friends, I start making excuses. It won't matter if I miss a session at the gym here, eat a fattening meal there. Then before I know it, I'm back to square one.

The issue is that I am not focusing on the purpose of my goal: the overall positive intent. Saying 'I will lose weight' is not enough. 'I am healthy and have the energy to live an abundant life' – now that goal is completely different. It is not solely about the weight, it is a lifestyle choice.

Determination is a good thing. It means that willpower will not be the only driver in achieving the goal. But we need to find ways to make it easy for ourselves to achieve what we want – for example, by creating milestones and rewards, journaling, and asking a friend/partner to provide constructive feedback.

Put all you can into achieving the success that you deserve.

Bumps in the road

We do not live in a static world. Life is an amazing gift and will always throw new things at us from which we can choose to learn and grow. Challenges and hardships are lessons, and the more challenges we face, the better we'll become at solving problems. But do not let them take your dreams away. There is no failure, only feedback.

I met with an old friend, Tony, a keen cyclist who had spent the last six months training for a week of racing in the Pyrenees. His determination was excellent, he had set goals, been diligent in his planning, and was very much looking forward to reaping the rewards of his labours.

Unfortunately, on the first stage of his seven-day race, he suffered significant cramps which delayed him by fifty minutes. But by the last day of racing, he felt confident that he had achieved the unachievable and caught up with the top 100. Unfortunately, just as the race was coming to a close, he suffered yet another setback with a mechanical fault on his bike.

Despite the setbacks, Tony only fell short of his goal by eight minutes. He was so angry and resentful that he decided he would not compete again. After all his efforts, he perceived his amazing achievement as a failure.

I am always saddened by stories of people simply giving up on their dreams due to some hurdle or other. Though the definition of success may vary from one person to another, I agree with this one:

'Success is the progressive realization of a worthy goal or ideal.'

EARL NIGHTINGALE

Finding the secret

Here is one more question to ask yourself while looking at your goal.

> *'Why live an ordinary life, when you can live an extraordinary one.'*
>
> ———
>
> **TONY ROBBINS**

Are you inspired by it?

> *'If your goals don't inspire you every day, you need a new set of goals.'*
>
> ———
>
> **D. THOMAS**

One of my most inspiring mentors talks about following your highest excitement in life, and I abide by this principle. Excitement could also be your biggest fear as long as following it will be a positive endeavour. Take calculated risks; break the boundaries of what you think is impossible.

I used to be scared of running my own business; I now have two. I used to be scared of heights; I've accomplished a tandem skydive jump. Now I can reason with my unreasonable fear of standing on top of a ladder. I even used to be scared of standing up to people, and compromised myself out of consideration for them. I now realise that taking the courage to speak up at the appropriate time and setting your own boundaries generates more fruitful and connected relationships with others.

The second piece of advice is to start right now. Not Monday or next week. Activate your RAS without delay to focus on the steps necessary to achieve what you want. Postponing it will just be procrastinating. Your dreams will remain dreams if you don't take action steps today.

If you are serious about your goals and your future, now is the time to take your passion and enthusiasm and put them to work for you. Once you take action, however small, you will get a feeling of great satisfaction and accomplishment. You will feel inspired to take the next action step that will bring you even closer to achieving your goals.

> *'You are the average of the five people you spend the most time with.'*
>
> ———
>
> **JIM ROHN**

I recommend that you surround yourself with positive thinking, action-orientated people who will push you and motivate you to achieve your goals. Make a list of who you surround yourself with. Are they positive influences in your life?

Help to keep yourself on track with your goals by writing each day in a personal journal. Make a note of your daily action steps and keep track of your positive progress. Remember, small daily steps will lead to massive results.

> *'Dreams don't work unless you do.'*
>
> ———
>
> **JOHN C. MAXWELL**

EXERCISE 3

Once you have set your goals, revisit them the next day and tweak them. You have a week to finalise your goals, so focus on them. What do you want and how are you going to get there?

Next week we will begin our journey towards making your goals a reality.

Week Two

It's Time To Let Go

Well done on completing the first week. This week is going to be a freeing week.

The key to your success is to focus on what you want – what matters the most to you. It is about making choices and prioritising. If you are dieting, for example, will you choose to eat that large slice of maple and pecan pie, or be healthier and more energetic in the long run?

There are no right or wrong choices, just educated ones.

Think back to where you were five years ago. What were the choices you made then that got you to where you are now? What key decisions did you make (or not make) that shaped your life as you know it today? Can you remember some of your goals and aspirations from back then? What do you know now that you did not know then? Are there any choices that you wish you had made? Any lingering goals?

Write all your answers down.

It's all about time

Time is an amazing thing. It whizzes by in a blink or drags on and on. So when we think of the small choices we make every day, they tend to dissolve into the ether that is time. And with careful consideration and attention, time can be on our side.

If I think about where my life was five years ago compared to today, I have some goals that have remained the same, but others do not matter any longer. Back then, I was in a secure and somewhat stressful corporate role and wanted more money, more possessions, more luxury trips. I had forgotten to look at what I actually needed, succumbing to ideas, ideals and lifestyle that others had imposed upon me. Then I jumped off the cliff (metaphorically, of course) and learned that I could fly.

Instead of wishing my life was more like this, or more like that, I take action each and everyday.

I personally love the analogy of life being like water. It constantly moves and takes different courses. Try to control its flow and you will find that you cannot. If you choose to stay stagnant in life, things may appear safe and secure for a while. Be aware that stagnant water can become putrid. Avoid becoming trapped in a routine which simply kills time. If you do not move at all, you may still be where you are now in two years, or five, or ten.

If you are stuck, it may be a good idea to observe what limiting beliefs you have, consciously or unconsciously. We will be dedicating some time to that this week.

P is for procrastination

In the age of instant communication, many of us have found ourselves being jerked around like puppets on a string. We respond to every ringing phone or instant message, and the result is a day filled with stop-start-stop-start activity.

> *'Don't confuse activity with accomplishment.'*
>
> ―――――――
>
> **ZIG ZIGLAR**

We then look back on a day and realise that we have been busy, busy, busy, but have accomplished nothing.

Any time we are moving through the day without focus, it almost always comes down to us being unclear about our priorities. If we stopped several times each day to ask ourselves, 'What is the purpose of what I am doing right now?' the answer would often be, 'I have no idea.' This is where perspective comes into play. I personally find that engaging in mindfulness/meditation practices helps me to pause and acknowledge the purpose of everything I am doing.

In my home, we have a mobile phone ban between 6.30 and 8.30pm. The other day, I forgot to switch my mobile phone to the silent mode, and when my phone started manically bleeping, indicating I had received some messages, I became distracted. What could the messages be? A dinner date with my girlfriends? A customer asking for some feedback? News on the contract that I have been waiting on for ages? A call from my family in France? The suspense was too hard for me to bear. That night, I failed to appreciate the meal that was in front of me or enjoy the banter with my family. What does this teach my children? That having a screen in front of me is more important than they are?

Today, my priority, my goal, is to engage with the present and nurture the relationships that matter to me. Being in the present is one of the secrets of true happiness.

This point is easily proven. Think of the last time you were truly and utterly happy. Were you experiencing conflicts in other areas of your life? Did you have time pressures, business deadlines and so on? Almost certainly, but what were you doing at that time?

Every single person I have asked this question agreed that they were completely in the present. They weren't thinking about the past or planning the future.

In short, once you have determined what your priorities are, commit to them. Make time for them. Then, once you have started working on one, refuse to be distracted by anything less than a true emergency until you are through.

Starting from where you are

I've come to realise that people only experience dissatisfaction with their life when they believe that their situation should be different. What we call 'the stress of life' rarely has anything to do with what's actually going on. As human beings, we don't experience the 'real world'; we experience our own interpretation of it, which is based on thoughts that come and go.

If we are unhappy with where we are right now, the cause of the feeling will be rooted in the thought that there is some other place we would rather be. There is another direction we are supposed to be heading in. The most stressful strategy we can adopt for motivating ourselves to change our situation in this case is to direct our emotional energy towards hating the way things are. We convince ourselves that if we can muster up a strong enough loathing for our current landscape, we will be compelled to take massive action.

Don't feel that you're alone if you've been adopting this approach, as most people have at one time or another. I often have stressful days juggling family life, children, customers and so on, struggling with an ever-growing list of conflicting priorities. It is only when I take time to stop, ground myself, and be present, even for five minutes, that I can truly see beyond the day-to-day chatter in my mind and focus on what will truly make it all worthwile. There are some sacrifices, of course, so always make sure that such sacrifices are worthwile compared to the greater cause.

One of the things that frustrates me most in one to one coaching sessions is when a client does not realise what amazing attributes and resources they already have. Over time, they have just got used to feeling bad. Their negativity has become habitual, which not only sets them on a path of blaming and complaining, it also shuts them off from the inspired thinking they need to turn their 'right here, right now' into something better.

I know how it feels to be negative and powerless; I know how suffocating your own thoughts can be. As the mother of young children and having limited sleep, I have definitely found myself in this place from time to time. Some situations or conditions such as PTSD have a way of making you feel completely powerless and at the mercy of your own thoughts, but remember, they are just that: a series of thoughts and feelings to which you can choose to pay attention.

Listen to your mind and your thoughts. There are no un-resourceful people, just un-resourceful states.

'No problem can be solved from the same level of consciousness that created it.'

ALBERT EINSTEIN

In my experience, there are three kinds of thought that can cause us to feel dissatisfied with where we are:

- Thoughts about expectation

- Thoughts about purpose

- Thoughts that anything would be better than where we are

Thoughts about expectation. All through our lives, we have had the bar set for us by our parents, teachers, friends, colleagues, advertisers, glossy magazines, and even ourselves with regards to the standards and accomplishments we should have reached. We measure the distance between who we think we are and who we think we should be, and then allow ourselves to become anxious about the size of the gap (or chasm, in some cases). Remember Liza in the previous chapter, living the life that her parents had wished for her?

Thoughts about purpose. This is where we feel that our circumstances and outside influences are preventing us from living the life we want to live, doing the things we want to do and making a positive difference to the world. We feel we are wasting our lives, leaving us stewing with frustration and resentment.

The most common reason these thoughts become an issue is because we make living our purpose dependent on a specific set of criteria. We cannot be truly happy until we have enough money/energy/creativity/opportunity/support/freedom. This is the best way to feel really frustrated with our lives.

Our purpose should be an easy path to follow. When I found mine, I felt like a weight had been lifted from my shoulders. I remember crying with amazement, wonder and excitement at my simple yet earth-shattering revelation.

'Anything would be better than this'. This thought crops up when we have no idea what we want. What we do know is that we're not having fun right now. This is actually when I am most excited for clients as they are on a significant path of change and discovery.

You are exactly where you are supposed to be. How do I know? Because you're not anywhere else. So what is the stress-free formula for turning 'right here, right now' into a place you love?

EXERCISE 4

There is a big difference between how you show up in the world when you are trying to prove the circumstances of your life are holding you back, and how you show up when you are coming from a place of inspired service. Service in this context simply means being the best version of yourself.

There are three questions to ask yourself to help things along nicely:

- How would you feel if 'right here, right now' were the happy place you want it to be?

- How would you think and behave with that feeling as your guide?

- How would you treat yourself and interact with others?

Write all your answers down, then add them into your life straight away.

The instant we assume the feeling of the wish fulfilled and operate from that space, we transform the present moment in the most wonderful ways. Initially, nothing will change and yet everything will feel different. With patience, we realise over time that not only can we go after whatever it is we want to create in our life, but we can remain happy, regardless of how the scenery changes along the way.

Think about the decisions you make every day and how they have one simple outcome. Sometimes it's about uttering a few words: 'I love you'; 'It's over'; 'I think we should stop'; 'This really sounds amazing'. Sometimes it's about taking action: decluttering your home; booking that once-in-a-lifetime trip; quitting your job; joining the gym. The smallest of decisions can have the most impact, just like the fluttering of a butterfly's wings can cause a tsunami.

Moving from where you are

Limiting beliefs and attitude play a leading role in whether you will fail or succeed. Here's what to watch out for and what to do when you see obstacles coming your way.

Monday. For most people, Monday means going back to work for another week. One thing that separates positive people from the majority of their co-workers is their approach to Mondays.

Make a point of greeting each of your colleagues by name with an upbeat 'Good morning'.

The reaction you get will probably be along the lines of 'Yeah, what's so good about it? It's Monday', or 'Same old, same old', or 'Could be better'. This negative response to your positive attitude implies that you must have forgotten which day of the week it is. Don't allow the negativity into the conversation, though. If you then ask your colleague how their weekend was, for example, word the question in a positive way.

'What happened that was good this weekend?'

I find it fascinating that my son never remembers what happened at school each day when I ask him. So instead, I ask him, 'What was your favourite part of today?' This then leads to a much more positive exchange where we truly connect on the topics that he loves.

You are given what you give. Be mindful of this every day – give positivity and it will come back to you.

The poverty cycle. What makes up the poverty cycle? People are either time poor, people poor, or money poor.

Time poor. Everybody has the same amount of time every day. What differs is how people use it. Where many tend to go wrong is in over-estimating how much time they have left to complete something, and under-estimating how long it will take. One way to overcome this is to develop the habit of being on time, or even early when possible. You cannot be successful and be a person who is late. If you are lacking in this area, develop the habit of promptness.

People poor. Happy couples say there are two key contributors to their happiness: trust and time together.

Schedule time to spend in your most important relationships. When you are spending time with family and friends, enjoy it. Have fun. As human beings, we often forget to be impulsive. Allow yourself to be creative and follow your impulses from time to time. An email or a letter can go a long way to building connections.

Money poor. People who are money poor often begrudge those who are wealthy, but almost 90% of wealthy people started from an average to poor background. They have earned their wealth fair and square.

Changing attitudes about money can be hard, even among people who have a decent job and a decent pay cheque. Whenever you hear someone making a comment about the financially well-off being greedy, dishonest, or lucky, do your best to express the contrary view.

Now take time to reflect on these three areas. Are you poor in any of them? Write down where you would like to focus your attention this week.

Limiting beliefs

Limiting beliefs limit you. A positive limiting belief is one that limits you from doing dangerous or bad things, for example, 'I don't touch hot stoves'. This is a limiting belief in that it keeps you from doing something, but in this case the limitation is good. However, a limiting belief can easily be negative, for example, 'I never trust people because they eventually stab you in the back' or 'I have PTSD'. Negative limiting beliefs are not always 100% rational, even though we may think they are.

How can we change negative limiting beliefs? Before we can change them, we have to know what our limiting beliefs or decisions are. Once we have identified them, we can analyse them and put them into one of two groups: positive or negative.

In the next week or so, pay attention to your internal talk and decisions, and write down your key limitations. An example is given below.

POSITIVE	NEGATIVE
Trust your inner self	I cannot lose weight

When you've recognised and grouped your limitations, figure out what the limiting belief behind each one is. The belief will come right after the word 'because', for example, 'I trust my inner self because it's the right thing to do' or 'I cannot lose weight because I have no willpower'.

Sometimes the underlying belief is easy to find; sometimes you need to ask the right questions: 'What is the purpose behind me thinking that way?'; 'What is it protecting me from?'; 'What is it limiting me from doing?'; 'Is this really the way I feel?'; 'What is it about this limitation that makes me feel right or wrong?'

When you have found the beliefs underlying your negative limitations, you can change them. For example, I often hear people say, 'I am not confident.' Do they have a definition of what it means to be confident, or is this belief self-imposed? If they know what being confident looks, sounds and feels like, then they can look for the confidence that is already within them. 'I never trust people because they eventually stab you in the back' can be changed to 'The best way to get to know someone is to trust them.'

Choice

The only way to get better at making choices that are right for you is to make more decisions, then learn from them. Don't be paralysed by indecision.

> *'In any moment of decision, the best thing you can do is the right thing, the next best thing is the wrong thing, and the worst thing you can do is nothing.'*
>
> ———
>
> **THEODORE ROOSEVELT**

Some decisions come in a flash of almost divine inspiration. My colleague Samantha recalled the moment she decided her marriage was over. She simply woke up one morning and that was that. Her whole self agreed that today was the day she would leave. And she has had no regrets since.

I personally do not believe that there are any wrong decisions. You may regret poor decisions and that's OK. The trick is to turn that regret into a lesson learned. If you make a decision that is so bad you cannot learn anything from it, pat yourself on the back because at least you did something. Remember that accepting your past is a key aspect of moving forward easily and effortlessly. Acceptance is not about agreeing with or letting go of what happened; it's about being open enough to see it for what it was, integrate it into your story, and enjoy learning lessons from it.

What will you do the next time you are faced with a difficult decision? The choice is yours.

Exercises for success

Imaginative exercises are useful for developing the natural creative powers we were born with. I marvel at the ability of children to move in and out of different worlds, expressing themselves effortlessly. To master your mind is to master your life, and the following imaginative exercises will help you do just that.

EXERCISE 5

The first exercise focuses on your surroundings. You can do this anywhere at anytime. Take morning rush hour, for example. I used to find that the busier the traffic around me was, the more irritated I became. I knew this wasn't anyone's problem but mine, so I decided that rather than continue to feel irritated, I would change my mood and start my day in a positive mindset. I did this by imagining what the road would be like if it were in the middle of a large forest. It'd just be me, my car and my thoughts. Then, piece by piece, I would erase all of the distractions around me. With a little practice, I was able to feel as comfortable in traffic jams as I would on a road by myself.

It is easy to focus on the causes of our discomfort when we are stressed, so try focusing on the opposite. Stop whatever it is that is stressing you and focus your attention on becoming ultra-sensitive to touch, for example. Feel the air on your face, the clothes that you are wearing. This technique can be used in countless ways, and the more you practise it, the more effective it will become for you. Your imagination is key, but what really makes this exercise work is to believe in what you are imagining. This causes you to feel the emotions tied to the mental images you are focusing on.

EXERCISE 6

The second exercise is basic, but it takes careful practice to develop it as a real skill. The people who succeed in this exercise seem to have an edge when it comes to creative visualisation and attraction.

Start by holding something common like a warm cup of tea. Remember its exact feeling. Focus on the details like the texture of the cup and the smell of the tea.

Now step away from the cup of tea and go into another room. Try to experience the exact sensations you had when you were holding the cup of tea without actually holding it. Take some time and relive the experience. Practise this until you cannot believe that it is not in your hands.

Try feeling random things with your mind from afar. It can be anything from your sofa at home to the fruit in the grocery store. Imaginative exercises like this one train your mental senses to create whatever you imagine. This strengthens the power and effectiveness of any goal.

My favourite imaginative exercise for success is based on the principle of positive attraction. It is a self-esteem tool modified to develop creative power.

The only way anyone can hurt you mentally and emotionally is if you allow it. They need your permission, because the only way another person's comment, look, or act can truly hurt you is if you believe you are the person they are showing you they think you are. This is why your friends and family can hurt you the most. You automatically believe them more than a stranger, and sometimes even more than yourself.

EXERCISE 7

When someone pushes your boundaries, there is no need to respond with the self-defence mechanism of anger or allow yourself to feel victimised. Diffuse the situation within your mind. Accept it and tell yourself that it does not matter as you are the only source of who and what you are. You will then have no reason to feel anger or hurt. Forgive the other person and offer kindness in return. This will be guaranteed to bring more positivity into your life.

This is probably the most difficult of the imaginative exercises. Accepting those who hurt us doesn't come naturally; it takes true strength and high self-esteem. Practise it and stick with it.

Mindfulness – the practice of being aware

A mindfulness exercise that can work for anyone is the age-old technique of paying attention to your breathing. The beauty of this simple exercise is that we are always breathing. Even in the most stressful circumstances, we cannot stop. In the midst of each activity, we can always pop back to paying attention to our breathing.

Mindfulness exercises are not intended to create a state of sublimity so much as a recollection of the intrinsic wonder of life. Each time life situations make you feel anxious and disconnected, simply practise stillness. Quietly concentrate on your slow and gentle inhalation and exhalation. Remind yourself that you are alive. Quieten the internal chatter and find your internal anchor.

There is a wide range of ways to practise mindfulness and I will share some with you. The key thing to take on board is just to do it – and keep doing it as much as you can. I often treat myself to mindful moments when washing up or doing other daily tasks, making sure that I become super aware of the moment, focusing on my breath, the sensations I can feel externally and internally, and quietening my thoughts.

Mindfulness exercises can be divided into activity-based exercises and observational exercises. Both types can be undertaken in groups or on your own.

Typical activity-based mindfulness practices include:

- Walking

- Physical exercises, e.g. tai chi

- Eating

- Household/domestic chores

- Outdoor tasks, e.g. gardening

- My son's favourite – playing with Lego

Typical observational mindfulness exercises include:

- Breathing

- Body awareness and deep relaxation

- Sitting meditation

- Mindful silence

- Mindful listening

Putting it into practice

In my experience, there is a great benefit in undertaking mindfulness exercises with other people. There is a strong energy to group activity, and this can be encouraging and helpful in your own practice of mindfulness. Being a mindfulness trainer, I am often amazed by the energy of the group and witness life-changing effects.

However, the real work is done on your own, and this largely falls into two categories.

Formal practice. This is where you apply regular focused attention to one or two mindfulness exercises at a time until you have mastered them and they have become habits. As with the acquisition of any new skill, this requires self-discipline, persistence and consistency.

Integration practice. This is where you take your newly acquired mindfulness skills and apply them at different times of the day. This may be situation specific, for example interaction with a colleague who irritates you. Applying mindfulness in relationship situations can be instructive and powerful, and over time can change the negative and destructive aspects of the relationship.

The other type of integration practice is state specific – this is where you mindfully monitor your internal states throughout the day.

EXERCISE 8

Take three minutes three times this week to sit and breathe at the end of each day. Think about how the day unfolded and how you played an active part in it. Make sure that you are not interrupted. I usually work back from the present time to the morning rather than start from my morning. I find the thread a lot more insightful.

Reflect on the key decisions you took or chose not to take. Were you active in your day or passive (either is OK)? Write down your findings.

Think of yourself as an energy tank. At the end of the day, are you able to retain your energy or increase it, or is it depleted? What contributed to filling or emptying the tank?

In our lives, we want to keep our energy tank full so that we can focus and achieve what we want. How we fill our tank depends on the decisions that we take. What makes us feel great?

For example, interactions with some indivduals will make me feel better than interactions with others. A negative interaction (for example, shouting at my son several times to put his shoes on) will deplete my energy tank, whereas a positive interaction (sitting down with my son and giving him the attention he needs) will refill it.

This week, write down all the key decisions you take throughout your day and notice how they impact the way you feel. Explore your thinking and discover the decisions that will propel you forward and those that will limit you. By the end of this week, make sure you have cleaned up a significant amount of the push/pull energy which ultimately depletes your tank.

Several years back, I suffered greatly from what I call 'not good enough syndrome'. This belief actually turned me into a high achiever as I felt the need to prove myself to everyone. On the other hand I could never voice my opinion, be assertive or set my own boundaries. I still felt I wasn't good enough deep down inside.

When I realised that I was worthy, that I had my place and purpose, I decided I could achieve anything I wanted. And still am today.

I also believed that I could not lose weight. When I was tired or angry, I would comfort eat, justifying my actions with the limiting belief that as I was unable to lose weight anyway, what harm could it do? I have changed my belief to 'I am healthy' (present tense) which allows me to treat myself from time to time while taking the pressure off my shoulders with regards to my body image.

It's all about the angle from which you view an issue. Look at your limiting beliefs and write down your breakthrough sentence. For example, change 'I am not good enough' to 'I am worthy of an excellent life', or 'I cannot lose weight' to 'I am healthy'.

Tender loving care

One day, I accidently cut in front of another driver. She hooted her horn and I felt really bad for not having seen her. Shortly afterwards, she overtook me with her window down and voiced her anger. That made me feel even worse. By the time I got home, I was feeling very bad about myself. My feeling bad didn't improve the situation at all; I was simply hurting myself while the other driver was long gone.

When we accidentaly cut a finger while chopping vegetables, the first thing we do is clean the wound and apply a plaster. What amazes me is that people don't seem to apply the same tender loving care when they hurt themselves emotionally.

Mindfulness is a way of training yourself to accept life as it is, not as you would like it to be.

EXERCISE 9

Close your eyes and sit up in a chair. Make sure your spine is straight. Take several deep, slow breaths and remove any tension from your body. Consciously relax every muscle.

Focus on the tip of your nose, paying attention to the process of inhaling and exhaling. Feel your breath move in and out of your body. As you do this, observe your thoughts without any attachment or judgment. See if you can allow your mind to settle into a place of inner stillness. Rest there for some time, not allowing your thoughts to pull you out of this awakened yet relaxed space.

Now, slowly shrug your shoulders and open your eyes.

Even if you only do this basic mindfulness exercise for ten minutes a day, it will have a profound impact on your daily life.

Negative energy

In my line of work, especially in human resources, I sometimes get to spend days working on unpleasant situations – from redundancies and disciplinary cases to dealing with harassment and so on. What I find is that this often breeds negative energy which, if I'm not careful, can seep into my home life. Recently I felt as if my body was carrying all the tension in the meeting room, even though I had just been sitting there as a witness. It took considerable effort to find myself again after being exposed to such negativity.

Negative energy is destructive. The negative energy between a fighting husband and wife will spread to their children, neighbours and in-laws. Negative energy between nations will lead to conflict. So how do we release the negative energy built up inside us so that it does not pollute the atmosphere?

Anger, resentment, hate, fear and similar emotions are negative energies. They lack something. Anger lacks kindness, resentment lacks acceptance, hate and fear lack love, so you can choose to fill the gap with the positive emotion that is lacking. Feed your anger with kindness, your resentment with acceptance, your hate or fear with love. Negative energies and emotions are going to impede your life if you do not dispose of them properly. And the only way to dispose of them properly is to put positive emotions and energy in their place.

Ultimately, the choice is always yours. You can choose to live positively or you can choose to live negatively.

EXERCISE 10

Sit with your feet on the ground and imagine that you are growing roots. At the same time, imagine a light thread keeping your head up with your chin slightly down.

As you breathe in, feel all the good energy from the earth – the energy that makes the plants grow, the birds sing, children laugh, etc. – and let it rise from the tip of your toes to your ankles. As you breathe out, send your negative energy back into the earth through your roots so it can be cleansed and recycled. Breathe in the good energy to your knees, then your waist, then your chest, and so on, all the while breathing out your negative energy into the earth until you feel that the weight of negativity has left your body.

Try this exercise several times this week and enjoy the experience of feeling clean again internally.

Week Three

Every Step You Take

As we know, Rome was not built in a day. Keeping a clear head, focusing on where we are going and how we will get there, is important to success.

> *'If you don't know where you're going, you will probably end up somewhere else.'*
>
> ———
>
> **LAURENCE J PETER**

Without a specific goal or perspective in your mind, life can seem meaningless. I meet many people who simply live on a day-to-day basis and accept that this is as good as things will get. Often this leads to depression, eating disorders, mental disorders, etc.

It takes a lot of courage to get yourself out of this state and take positive action. Success comes to those who dream, plan and strive for it. Only if you have your eye on the prize will you get your hands on it in the end.

Goals can range from something as basic as getting up early in the morning to something as complex as climbing the success ladder. It can be as simple as being able to stand on your own two feet for the first day back at school. No matter how big or small your goal is, the key to achieving it is the right kind of attitude. For people suffering from depression, for example, simply getting out of bed in the morning can be a significant step towards a better tomorrow.

When I finally came to my breaking point, realising that my life had emptied itself of meaning, I went through a phase of complete overwhelm, not knowing what to change first. This overwhelm led me to a stalemate in which I worried that any particular move would make whatever I still held dear collapse completely. I slowly came to the understanding that to live a life of purpose didn't require me to shave my head, move to a convent, and dedicate myself to a life of spiritual growth.The life I had already built could be tweaked and enhanced to enable me to follow my own journey; I was already on the path and did not need to create a new one.

Your attitude governs your perspective, your thinking and your behaviour throughout life, and how you see and react to a situation in your daily routine. The right kind of attitude encourages positivity, hope and motivation, and paves the way to success. Taking the decision to lead a more positive life is easy, but making it a reality requires deep awareness of the work going on inside you. Once you have the right kind of attitude, your way forward will be clear and you are far more likely to accomplish your goals.

Whatever your goal may be, be proactive and plan each step. Those who plan ahead are aware of what lies in store for them and how they can best cope with the challenges of life.

Once you are on your way to success in accomplishing your goals, do not forget to breathe some energy into the ultimate destination once in a while. You may encounter disappointments in life, but do not let them hinder your desire to make your dreams come true. Those who rise from disappointments are more prone to achieving success in their life because they are open to learning lessons and overcoming challenges.

Think positively, be proactive and get productive today. It is not impossible or difficult to turn your dreams into reality and make success come naturally to you. With the right kind of attitude, you can set your life on a different footing whenever you want.

> *'Shoot for the moon. Even if you miss,*
> *you'll land among the stars.'*
>
> ————————
>
> **LES BROWN**

Do you know where you're going?

If you don't want to keep going round in circles, you need to have a plan, which includes revisiting where your past led you. Don't be afraid to face your past. It will help you build a future.

One mistake I've observed people making is that they want to leave the past behind without confronting the consequences caused by previous behaviour. This is one of life's biggest challenges. It takes an incredible amount of patience, persistence, self-love and will to look at the cycles of the past and learn lessons from them. Although it may take time to work through, if you stay stagnant, you won't see the results you are hoping for. My past is still vivid, and I carry it with me. What has changed is that I have attached a lot less meaning to it, dedicated less energy to ruminating on it, which allows me to reinvest myself in building my future.

You will know you're heading in the right direction when you see different results. In the past, if there were painful consequences when you behaved in a certain manner, that indicated a problem. With a change of thinking and behaviour, you will make choices that lead to a fruitful outcome. For me, this meant taking back control of my life and at the same time surrendering to what my purpose is. It was about acceptance of the past and taking it as my personal strength rather than a weight on my shoulders. It was determination backed up with action. My greatest pain became my greatest driver. If I can face my fears and look at them as opportunities, then you can too.

It's time to be more than average. Decide that moulds and norms are not how you will benchmark yourself. You are an amazing being and owe yourself all of your deepest desires.

Knowing where we're going is the most direct way to get there. Yet sometimes we just don't know. We still have old 'stories' swimming around in our head – 'You should be like this'; 'What will Aunty So-and-so make of what you have just done?'; 'You can't possibly contemplate achieving this by yourself'; etc. Therefore, we are limited in the options we'll allow ourselves to entertain. The stories keep us stuck, just like limiting beliefs and decisions.

Here is a process to help you know where you're going. This process will support you in finding your purpose and aligning your goal with that.

What can you say for certain that you want in life? You don't have to know the whole picture; start with something small. Maybe you want to travel more, spend more time with friends or family, take classes, or have a home with a view. Perhaps you want an inspiring relationship, or a career that capitalises on your creativity. Choose the thing you're clear about and focus on that.

What we focus on grows. Think about the thing that you want and the purpose around you wanting it. What will it do for you? Imagine yourself having it in your life. What is life like then? How does it make you feel to have it?

Spend time each day thinking about that thing and being grateful in advance for the fact that it is in your life. If you can imagine it, it is possible.

When you focus on the thing you want, you are not simply wishing and hoping. If you do it well, you will be mentally putting yourself there, instantly shifting your energetic state to one of love, possibility and passion. When you are in a passion-driven state, it is fun. Focusing on what you desire as if it is already here makes you happy.

When you're in this energy state, more of what you really want will reveal itself. You have removed yourself, mentally and energetically, from fear-based concerns (e.g. 'What if?' and 'Not enough' thinking), and your intuitive genius will emerge. Focus on what you desire, then look around. What opportunities do you see for action towards your goal? Again, picture yourself with the end goal achieved. What else do you notice about what your life looks like? Where are you? Who is around you? What work are you doing? What relationships do you enjoy? Trust these observations and write them down.

If you continue this process over time, you will build a clear picture of where you are going, and you'll be on the road taking you there.

I often find that my motivation is super high when it comes to setting goals, and the first couple of weeks are usually easy as my resolve to achieve what I want is strong. Then I start experiencing my first successes, achieving my first milestones, and I become somewhat complacent. The next section will show you exactly how to keep yourself on track.

The Way to Success

The Way to Success is a method for improving your success in a systematic way. By making the approach explicit, we can improve it and fine tune it to achieve better, faster, and simpler results. The beauty of the Way to Success is that we can enjoy the journey towards achieving our goal as well as the destination.

Here are the key steps to the Way to Success:

Step 1: Imagine the future. This is the most important step. It is about painting a picture of the future with enough clarity and conviction that it creates a burning desire.

By now, you should have a vivid mental model of the future. Your mental model will guide your actions, thoughts, and feelings. The richer your mental model, the easier it will be for your mind to get creative in finding ways to make your vision a reality.

Another important reason for clarity in your mental model is to reduce conflict. If your mind, heart, body, and spirit want the same things, then you have all of you working on your side. A fractured or conflicting vision will fork your focus, fork your energy, fork your priorities, and make anything you do ten times more difficult. When all of you is fully aligned, you fire on all cylinders and make things happen.

Step 2: Map out the goals. This breaks your vision down into achievable steps and results. As a suggestion, you can write down the wins you want as simple one-liner statements. By keeping your goals lightweight to begin with, you can evolve them as you get a better idea of what success will actually look like. It's like a picture slowly coming into focus.

Step 3: Model the best. In this step, find the best stories, people, and examples to model your success on. You can then use the examples to inspire and guide yourself with skill. They will help you avoid dead ends and glass ceilings.

In the NLP Master Practitioner programme that I run, participants are asked to spend some time identifting a person they want to learn a skill from. When they choose the person they are going to model themselves on, they make sure they choose the best.

When I was working on my corporate brand, I followed the example of the general manager of an organisation I had had the privilege to work with. To me, she had it all: the stamina, the work/life balance, the respect, and the poise that I was seeking. I did not ask her to become my coach or mentor (which would have been a perfectly acceptable thing to do); I simply asked myself in various situations, 'How would she react? What choices would she make?' I was able to make these decisions my own after several months of practice.

One of the best ways to speed up success is to build on the patterns and practices that work. Success always leaves clues. You can learn from the success of others to tune and prune your own success path.

Step 4: Test your results. In this step, you take action. Taking action will produce results, and as you produce results, you'll get feedback.

Test your results to find the best paths forward. As you take action, you may be surprised as new opportunities, new doorways, and new possibilities unfold. As my friend's father put it, 'Luck is when skill and opportunity come together.' By taking action and testing your results, you're increasing your luck.

Step 5: Change your approach based on feedback. This is where your 'tests for success' help you see whether you are getting closer to or further from what you want to accomplish.

A simple question to ask yourself here is, 'Is this effective?' If the actions you are taking are not effective, go back to your models, find insight, and change your approach.

When you take action, you produce results. The results will be leaving clues and insights, so use these to do more of what's working and less of what's not working, or to change the approach altogether. As obvious as it sounds, sometimes the best approach is to do the opposite of what's not working.

If you're working with mentors, you can share the approaches you have tried and the results you've got with them. An experienced mentor will then help you evaluate your results and identify alternative strategies or tactics. If you're not getting the results you want, it can be helpful to ask 'How?' questions instead of 'Why?' questions. When you ask 'How?' questions, you engage your brain in a more resourceful way and it starts helping you find a way.

A simple way to remember the Way to Success is: dream it, plan it, do it.

An ingredient for success

What is the most important ingredient for success? Is it having a mentor who can guide you through all the varying issues so you don't make any mistakes? Is it having powerful friends, relatives, or neighbours who can provide you with a high-paying position? While these could be the route for some, they won't help you achieve personal and professional success in the long run. What will is preparation.

> *'Find a job you enjoy doing,*
> *and you will never have to*
> *work a day in your life.'*
>
> ———
>
> **MARK TWAIN**

Thousands of people wish that they were able to do something they like to do. You can, but you won't be able to without preparation. To take advantage of opportunities when they are available, you have to be prepared. This preparation may mean higher education, specialised training, having enough money in the bank to buy a business, or establishing partnerships that help you obtain a position that requires sponsors. It may also mean having a detailed action plan written down in order to set the direction and actions you need to accomplish what you want. Whatever works for you.

Remember to celebrate when you reach milestones on your journey. Some people prefer to celebrate only once they have achieved their goals, but now it's time to be positive, selfish, excited and reflective all at once. The celebration needs to be pleasurable but not excessive. You want to feel good so that you are inspired to carry on, but you do not want to go overboard. Sometimes the celebration could be a reward, for example, 'If I reach a particular milestone, I will treat myself'. Small milestones have small rewards, while significant milestones deserve significant rewards.

This week, review all of your notes so far. Using a different colour pen, add comments, questions, insights and feedback to your journaling activity. Keep it positive. If you have fallen down at some point, offer yourself a note of recognition, give yourself the space to heal, appreciate your inner voice and stand back up, firmer than ever.

In my line of work, I may lose a contract or a bid. Those days are never great days to be around me. I am stressed, distracted, and struggle to focus on the task at hand, let alone positive thoughts. Over time, I have learned to appreciate these days as they teach me what it is that I want and how to get there. In the grand scheme of things, a lost contract does not matter. Instead of stressing, I book a day off to reflect and be grateful for the opportunity to learn.

How to overcome stress

Stress is a debilitating condition that can stop you in your tracks. Many in the scientific community now believe that the vast majority of diseases and sicknesses are caused by prolonged stress. Dr Mayo from the Mayo Clinic believes that many people have died because of worry. While it doesn't directly kill them, it leads to circulation problems, organ problems, cancer, and many other conditions. The majority of people in the world have no idea that they are killing themselves. They have no idea how to overcome stress, and they don't even know that they need to.

The funny thing about stress is that it is completely in the mind of the person who is suffering from it. While it may seem like our boss, spouse, or kids are making our lives stressful, they aren't. Nothing can make us stressed without our permission. Our reaction to the situation is what creates stress. Once we realise this, we are well on our way to learning how to overcome stress.

The trick is to make a conscious decision not to allow ourselves to get stressed. There are many techniques to use, breathing techniques, mindfulness, visualisation, and yoga being a few common ones. Concentrating on your logic is another great way to stop yourself being dragged into stress.

When something happens that would normally make you mad, ask yourself, 'Is getting stressed about this situation going to help anything? Am I even going to remember this ten years from now?' When you step back and look at your situation from another point of view, you tend to see how trivial it really is.

When we learn how to overcome stress, we realise that it is mainly a choice that we make every day. We can decide whether to allow stress to affect us or not. Everyone can overcome it. We simply need to know exactly what to do and how to do it.

Learn to relax. It took me a while to understand that relaxation isn't about letting go. It is about finding some space and stillness to let your unconscious mind do its most important work.

For many people, relaxation is something they do at weekends, or when they take a holiday. If you are under stress, however, it can't be put off. In fact, it's a good idea to practise it on a regular basis.

On a personal level, I find that twenty minutes of meditation each day before work works for me, as does regular tai chi practice. Relaxation doesn't need to involve a trip to the spa, candles, or a night out with friends. It can be something as simple as putting on your running shoes and going for a run, or calling a dear friend. Crucially, it involves being present in the moment.

The first thing to train yourself to do is to respond calmly to everyday stresses. Frustration will get you nowhere; accept whatever comes and adopt a flexible approach. The more flexible and adaptable you are, the easier life will be for you.

Consciously slow down, bringing in one thought at a time. When you feel stress building, you need a 'quiet room' or 'secret garden' in your mind – a place you can retreat to. Sit down in a favourite chair. Mentally repeat to yourself, 'I feel relaxed,' letting the tension go out of your muscles as you do this. Relieving the tension in your muscles is important because relaxed muscles lead to a relaxed mind.

Meditation. You can take relaxation a step further by using meditation. When you meditate, you clear your mind and pay attention to your breathing. Get comfortable in a chair, then take a deep breath and let it out slowly. It's important to make sure you breathe from your abdomen, not your chest. Keep your eyes closed as you relax.

Now, start at the top of your head and progressively relax each part of your body one at a time. Think about it, then let it relax. Feel your face – your forehead, cheeks and jaw. Let them get heavy and drop as you continue concentrating on your breathing. Move down to your neck and shoulders. Picture the muscles in them, let them get heavy and fall.

Relax them as much as possible, then go further and relax them more.

Beginning with your upper arms, picture yourself squeezing them. Let them get heavy, then let go. Relax them, then relax them further. Continue down to your chest and back; let them get heavy, then relax. Enjoy the tranquility of the moment as you continue breathing slowly in and out. Now move down to your stomach and hips. Relax them as much as possible, then relax them more. Finally do the same with your legs and feet.

Your entire body should be relaxed now. Continue breathing in and out slowly as you try to relax your body even more.

Positive thinking. Around 90,000 thoughts pass through our heads every day, and it has been estimated that up to 70% of them (for most people) are negative. And most of the stress we experience comes from negative thoughts.

Recognise these thoughts as negative immediately, and get rid of them. Don't stop to analyse them, just accept them as thoughts that come and go. It's a good idea to have a stockpile of positive thoughts ready. A few examples are thoughts of your family, your goals, or happy times you have had recently.

Exercise. Exercise stresses your muscles and body, so it may seem strange that it is good for combatting stress. But it may be one of the best things you can do if you are stressed. As you exercise, your mind calms. You are thinking only of the exercises you are doing, and not about your problems. Exercise also reduces anxiety and stimulates 'feel good' endorphins. After a good workout, you feel a glow that can last for hours.

Aerobic exercises are best for combatting stress as they get your heart beating. Walking is particularly good, but swimming, biking and rowing are excellent, too. It's also good to do weights, which build muscle and strengthen your bones. In just a few weeks, you will feel better and have more energy. Exercise keeps your blood pressure low, helps you lose weight and aids good quality sleep.

Sleep. Sleep deprivation is one of the greatest stressors. Most people need at least seven hours a night.

You may find it more difficult to get to sleep when you are stressed, so wind down before you go to bed. Take a warm bath or read a book until you are drowsy. Some other things you can do to sleep better are:

- Create a restful environment. Keep the bedroom at a comfortable temperature, and chose good quality mattress, pillow and sheets

- Go to bed at the same time each night, and rise at the same time each morning

- Exercise (but not just before you go to bed)

- Avoid anything that will disrupt your sleep, for example caffeine in the evening or long naps during the day (twenty minutes should be the maximum)

Diet. Stress is caused by poor diet, so make sure you get sufficient vitamins and minerals. The B vitamins are particularly good for combatting stress, and Vitamin C is needed for a healthy immune system. Vitamin D is also helpful.

Pay particular attention to vegetables, fruits, and grains. Some of the most nutritious are broccoli, tomatoes, carrots, beans, blueberries, oranges and grapefruit, oats and whole wheat. Also important are nuts, yogurt and milk, fish, turkey and chicken, eggs, soy and tea. Too much saturated fat in the diet can cause stress, as can too much coffee. Be careful of alcohol and drugs, too, as these may provide an instant fix, but will deplete your energy.

Friends and family. It's important to have people to talk to about your feelings. Sharing your problems almost always makes you feel better, and friends and family can offer encouragement and support.

People under stress tend to curtail their social life. This is a mistake. Mixing with people relieves stress, so get out and have fun – enjoy yourself. Do things with people you enjoy being around, but avoid any people who tend to stress you.

Humour. Laughter is an effective stress-reducer. Not only does it make you feel good, but it's fun. A belly laugh is particularly good. It relieves muscle tension, and helps your respiratory system and heart. When you are under stress, your adrenal glands release cortisol, and it's important to keep it under control. Studies have shown that laughter reduces cortisol. It also stimulates the immune system.

Simplify and organise your day. A major stressor for many people is their busy lifestyle. They are trying to squeeze too many things into their day, and on top of this, many are disorganised.

If this describes you, think about how you can cut back on some of your activities and organise others better. Time management is important, and the best way to deal with it is to have realistic goals. It's good to be ambitious, but being overwhelmed, with little or no rest, will cause stress. Aim at achieving one personal success a day. This can be as simple as taking 10 minutes to yourself.

Breaking your tasks down to manageable ones and tackling them one at a time in an organised way will help. And don't worry about them; worry causes stress.

Music. Listening to music relaxes you and makes you feel good. The problem with music is that everyone has different tastes, so be sure to select something that appeals to you. Then sit in a comfortable chair, lean back and let your favourite music wash over you. Feel yourself relax.

Playing a musical instrument is extremely relaxing, as is singing. Singing on karaoke or joining a choir are excellent ways to release stress.

Visualisation can be combined with music or done alone. The idea is to focus your mind on a pleasant and peaceful setting – a relaxing scene. It may be a beach or a mountain stream, or you could relive the enjoyment of an event you recently attended. Breathe slowly and regularly as you take in the image. Picture yourself lying on the beach watching the clouds drift overhead, listening to the waves rolling in, feeling the warmth of the sun on your skin, tasting and smelling the salty air.

Manage anger. When you feel anger coming on, control it quickly. Anger can increase and prolong stress, and it certainly triggers it.

One of the best ways to control anger is to take a deep breath, then relax as you breathe out. Continue breathing in and out as you count to ten. If this doesn't work, try exercising for several minutes, or listen to music. Calm yourself down before the anger gets out of control.

Practise patience. This is closely associated with managing anger. Become more tolerant of yourself and situations over which you have no control. Don't worry about them. Accept things as they are, and don't insist that everything must be the way you want it to be.

Without patience, you will be easily annoyed, irritated and frustrated, which will eventually lead to stress. Patience gives you inner peace and contentment, so don't let little things bother you.

Accept change. Change comes with life. Some changes, such as disappointments and losses, are not pleasant. People feel more comfortable with familiar people, places and situations, and changes of any kind can upset them. They may find it difficult and stressful to adjust.

To avoid stress, learn to accept change. View it as an opportunity for growth.

Reaching a success milestone may mean that you will eventually encounter stress. How is stress possible when you are successful? Stress from success may be encountered in the form of too many demands on your physical or overall well-being. Sometimes, success means that it's time for you to step away or reduce your involvement.

You're probably familiar with stories of successful entrepreneurs who, after having reached the financial pinnacles in their life, revamp their next steps so that they can enjoy a new level of happiness and joy. This may mean anything from stepping back to retirement, or volunteering their knowledge to help others less fortunate. Be prepared. Success is not one specific goal; success is more a journey that visits different ports along the way.

The power of success

When you start experiencing success, it is important not only to celebrate what you have achieved, but also to focus on what is still to come. Reaching a serious goal is going to require serious effort, and it is not a straight line progress. It is full of ups and downs, progress intermixed with regression. Sheer willpower and strength of personality are often not enough to achieve a goal.

Reaching a milestone provides you with two sources of energy. You feel good about your progress, and this feeling can give you confidence and energy to move towards the next milestone. And reaching a milestone is an accomplishment in itself, so celebrate and reward yourself. Each milestone is the end of a clearly defined stage of activity, and reaching the milestone means you have completed that particular part of the path to your goal. For example, when I am hiking, I define clearly recognisable landmarks on the trail as milestones. When I reach that milestone, I have completed a defined part of the hike.

Milestones also provide proof that you can be successful. After all, the milestone is a success in itself. This can give you the confidence you need to continue towards the overall goal.

Life is a set of milestones – one after the other. Small or large, challenges are there to be completed. I often find that when I focus on my milestones, tweaking and updating them, I actually overachieve them. The best plans are those that have been worked out, but it's also nice to be impulsive and creative around them.

Recently I decided that instead of writing down my milestones, I would create a mood board. This now has pride of place in my kitchen, reminding me of where I am going and the path that I have chosen to get me there.

Life is not always perfect (my mood board is far from being perfect, or even 100% clear), but neither am I.

Take a look at the milestones you still have to reach. Are they appealing? Have they changed?

My friend Jessica recently set herself a goal of losing weight after having had a baby. She gave herself six months to get there. For some reason, although she followed a carefully conceived meal plan, the weight did not come off.

The six months deadline arrived. Jessica had had a vivid image in her mind of being at a friend's wedding in a marvellous black and white dress of a certain size. She still went to the wedding, but in a blue dress. And she felt great in it. Although she had not achieved her original goal, she had taken steps towards a healthier lifestyle, exercising regularly and eating healthy meals. She felt more confident and at ease with her body image.

Was this a goal/milestone achieved? I would believe that yes, it was in a way. Being in the right mindset and knowing she has not given up will make Jessica's journey towards her goal easier than before.

Road map to success

Picture yourself in the final days of your life. Reflect back on your achievements and decide if they are what you hoped for. If your current achievements do not satisfy you, change the life you imagine. Add things that you would like to be able to say you have done when the end eventually comes. Get your ideas on paper.

Some examples include travelling the world, sky diving, owning a business, having kids, or being on television.

Once you have your goals, you can start to refine them.

Backwards plan. What will you need to achieve each goal by the time you are thirty, forty or fifty? It could be:

- A certain amount of money

- A certain income

- A certain type of employment or self-employment

- A passport

- A healthy lifestyle

- More confidence

- A partner

- Better image

List your ideas, then refine them. For example, to achieve each item on your list, you may need:

- A financial plan

- Further education

- To own the family home

- To pay off the car

And so on. Eventually, each large task becomes a series of small, achievable tasks.

Remember, we are mapping out potentially twenty to fifty years of your life. It is not due in for marking tomorrow. The key is to start with the small, achievable things that you could do without too much commitment.

For example, your first goal towards fitness may be to create a list of local gyms or not to eat takeaway at lunchtime more than once this week. When you take some form of action, you will get closer to your goals every day, and then one day you will find you have completed them all.

Momentum takes over with every step you take. If you improve your position by 1% every day, it will only take 100 days to achieve 100% of your goal. Would you prefer to receive £1 million in one go, or start with one penny which would be doubled daily for a month? If you took the penny, you would end up over £4 million better off.

If you struggle to get creative, open a catalogue and circle the material things you want in life. Do not be ashamed about wanting everything you see. Have fun with this; you can refine the things you want in order of importance later.

As you perform this process, daydream about the things that you do not have. You may find you're still circling products and turning pages, but you won't remember the last thing you looked at.

This is a good sign. We do not find everything we want in life in a catalogue. The technique is designed to gain access to the parts of ourselves that we generally do not show to the world. We all deserve everything that we want, but have been taught not to be greedy. As we move through different stages in our lives, we encounter all sorts of self-esteem battles and learn to settle for what life puts in front of us.

Do not give up on goal setting as it is fundamental to achieving success and fulfilment, as long as you keep an eye out for the things you do that could potentially delay or diminish your ability to reach the goal.

Listing your goals

When you list your major goals from all areas of your life, for example family, finance, health, career, etc., think of the greatest possibilities that the world has to offer. Why would you want to achieve the goal? Keep asking yourself what the purpose of your goal is until you cannot ask it any more. You will then have your long-term goal and the reason to overcome obstacles.

Ask yourself, 'If I could have one of these goals realised in the next twenty-four hours, which one would it be?' Whichever goal you decide on is the one to promote to the top of your list and focus on.

Then list your minor goals that are geared towards achieving your major goals. These minor goals should be small, short-term goals. Review your goals daily. Keep them in your mind. Focus on the positive reasons behind the goal, and not negativity or failure. Keep faith in them and they will remain clear. Creativity will provide you with the way if you feel like you're about to give up, so do not allow anyone or any obstacle to dampen your passion for success.

Set more and more goals. As you achieve them, add new ones. Do not wait or shortlist.

Believe in yourself. There is nothing on this earth that you do not deserve or are not capable of achieving, so take action, no matter how minute.

Most people think of goals as lofty expectations for the future, but goals don't have to be about a final result. Goals can be used to make every day more productive and efficient in a number of ways.

Focus. Goals focus you. It is easy to sit down at work, look at a messy desk and huge to-do list, and then procrastinate. But if you have written down specific goals for the day and you have them right in front of you, you know where to start and it's much easier to get the focus you need to have a productive day.

When you write goals for the day, it will force you to choose those that are important. Every to-do on your list has a level of importance, but note that the most productive people choose the ones that will make the most impact.

Accomplishment. At the end of the day, are you more frazzled and overwhelmed than when you started it?

Setting goals at the beginning of the day gives you something to achieve and be proud of. If you can look at your list of goals and put a tick next to them all, you will leave work with a sense of accomplishment and a spring in your step.

Advancement. Study after study has shown that people who set goals get more done and are more successful in every aspect of their lives than those who do not set goals. If you want to be promoted or successful in business, goals are imperative. If you leave work every day having achieved real results, people will notice and you will get ahead.

Time. People who set goals actually end up having more free time than those who don't, as the focus that you gain allows you to get your work done quickly. This means more time for family, hobbies and other passions outside of work, which has an effect on your attitude, refreshes you and allows you to return to work with renewed vigor.

Every Sunday evening, I plan the week ahead, including my own activities and meetings, my children's activities and groups, and our social events as a family. After that, I will list between three and five goals that will help me advance towards my greater goal.

Daily goals that get me through the moment are important. I get an incredible amount of well-being once they have been taken care of. For example, if I make a phone call I have been putting off, it may only take five minutes, but it will get rid of a lot of procrastination and negative vibes.

Give yourself more time, more focus, more accomplishment, more advancement, and get the important things done with daily goals

EXERCISE 11

Sit for ten minutes or so and view all the milestones you have accomplished. Take the time to notice any changes that may take place in your body. Sense check what has shifted and where more of a shift needs to take place.

Now focus on the achievement of your goal. Where else do shifts need to take place? What else needs to happen? Can you still see, hear, feel your end result? Is it vivid and appealing? Remember to tweak those submodalities to make it just about right.

Reward yourself. You have now completed twenty-one days of your seven week challenge. Make the most of this time to renew your commitment to you.

Week Four

You Can Make Your Dreams Come True

So that you have full congruency and clarity in terms of what you want, it's time to enhance your goals – make them so appealing that they become a no brainer (no pun intended). It's time to blend all of the good work you have achieved so far and continue training your mind to align everything in the right direction for you.

Working on your goal helps you adjust it until you get it right for you. Remember this journey is one of deep intrinsic change. Enjoy it as you move closer to what you want.

Sometimes the adjustment will be minimal, yet still a significant move forward. When I chose to stop smoking, for example, each cigarette that remained unlit was a small yet gigantic step towards a healthier and better smelling version of me. I prepared myself prior to going to a place where I would usually smoke, taking time to focus on what I wanted, and that simple new behaviour helped me to kick a long-term habit.

Reflect on the last three weeks. How are you doing with your goals? What are you accomplishing that you were not three weeks back? What has changed? What do you have left to achieve? What tweaks do you require? Be honest with yourself, and write all your ideas down. And remember there is no failure, only feedback.

Creating clear goals is one of the most essential ingredients to personal and professional success, so make them appealing to you and your unconscious. What I like to do after having tried and tested new behaviours for a couple of weeks is to align them with the end game. To achieve the results you want, you have to know your purpose, and that's where effective goal setting comes into play. According to *The Power of Focus* by Jack Canfield, Mark Victor Hansen and Les Hewitt, your goals should be:

- Yours

- Meaningful

- Specific and measurable

- Flexible

- Challenging and exciting

- Aligned with your core values

- Well-balanced

- Contributing to society

- Realistic

- Supported

Most of this we have already worked on in the last three weeks, which is great news.

Now that you have set your goals and decluttered your path towards achieving them, you need to determine exactly when you want to achieve them. A seven-week time frame is good because it's not too long, while allowing you enough time to establish some significant targets. As we learned in the previous chapter, having milestones within that time frame makes it simple to track your progress.

One of my clients, Kate, had a goal of being more confident, especially in the workplace. She had an incredible amount of passion and energy, but she was plagued with a poor self image. After having had three children she no longer had the physique she once had and kept talking about 'When I lose the weight...' This significantly slowed down her progress, putting all of her plans on hold: 'I will be more confident once I lose the weight.' We agreed that it was both ambitious and do-able to work on her personal image, focus on a healthier lifestyle, and encourage her to have more fun with her children, including accompanying them to the swimming pool – something she had never done. Then we worked on visualisation techniques. Kate increased her level of confidence, went shopping for a swimsuit, and planned her regular outing. She did not lose any weight in that first week, or even month. However, she made a significant step towards enjoying a more fulfilled life and grew in confidence at the same time. Having clear goals, a good plan, and someone to challenge her while ensuring the process was enjoyable, definitely gave her the results she deserved as well as a clearer vision of how she could link her future to taking action today.

You can achieve whatever results you have set your mind on in a simple and exciting way, too. If you keep working on various facets of your goals, remaining persistent and patient, you'll find yourself achieving one victory after another. Over time, you'll become an expert at flexing your goal muscles. The more you achieve your goals, the more motivated you will be to achieve the next one; then you'll enjoy more balance in your personal and professional life as you will be getting what you want easily and effortlessly.

> *'We don't know who we are*
> *until we see what we can do.'*
>
> ———————
>
> **MARTHA GRIMES**

Boosting your goals

In my line of work as a human resources professional, I am often baffled at discussions I hold with disgruntled employees. They will come to me saying things such as, 'My manager never gave me the promotion I worked so hard for', or 'I have been waiting for a pay rise for years'.

When I ask whether they have spoken to their manager about their desires, I am often faced with an expression of shock and horror.

The same happens in a relationship. Unfortunately, my partner isn't psychic. If I would like something to happen, I need to tell him. I was chatting with my friend Amelie yesterday evening about the fact that her husband had to work late on her son's birthday. She was upset by that, and quite rightly rather angry. When I asked her whether she had told her husband that she was expecting him to be home early so that they could enjoy a family evening in, she went quiet.

Waiting for things to happen simply slows down the process, which in turn slows down your journey. We cannot expect others to guess what we want. Expecting others to do something for us without giving them the chance to know what it is will generate anger, resentment, etc.

Success rarely happens by accident. Using goal setting to achieve your heart's desire will take effort, assertiveness, honesty and complete openess. Get rid of the erroneous belief that advancement in life is a slow and tedious process. It can be as easy as making a decision, picking up the phone, buying a book, etc.

In Week One, we set our goals. Now we are making them more vibrant, more compelling so that our conscious and unconscious minds can reach in their direction easily and effortlessly. Communicate with your support network what your goals and expectations are. Nurture the key relationships in your life, as they will nurture you in return.

Two weeks on from Week One, are there cracks appearing in what you set yourself to do? Has it been easier or harder than you planned? There often comes a point where we feel deflated, so any time you are starting to lose your grip on your goal, this will be the chapter to return to. It's time to make the magic work for you again and again.

I remember setting myself goals in my twenties. To date, I have achieved one of those goals, and that was easy to achieve. I have wasted a lot of time buying self-help books without reading them; making a decision to stop smoking without preparing myself; training for a half marathon without understanding the work required; and most all, ignoring those internal signs and simply keeping busy.

As you think about your goals, do you want to get better results? When you set your goals, did you really want to achieve them? How about in a week or two's time? How will your motivation be then? Is your motivation both strong enough and emotionally compelling enough to enable you to be successful? Is your motivation encouraging and supporting the personal behaviour changes required to overcome the obstacles that will inevitably rise up to thwart your efforts? Now is the time to supercharge your goal to make it so compelling that your motivation becomes unwavering.

I'm personally excited to share this particular part with you as it has made a difference to me and my clients over time. I struggled for years to stop smoking. I just couldn't stop – I was addicted (what a great example of a limiting belief) so I chose to light up one more time.

The minute I realised I was pregnant with my first child, I didn't drink a drop of alcohol or have a single cigarette. The idea of protecting my unborn child from harm was more compelling than a cigarette. Stopping smoking became easy and effortless. Each day, I had complete control over whether or not I would bring a cigarette to my lips. I chose my own freedom and finally disregarded the concept of addiction.

Of course, it was not easy. There were symptoms of physical dependency, but I used techniques to help me overcome these. Each one of us is different, but what is common to us all is the freedom of choice. Sometimes, the ultimate destination is worth the habitual change. My purpose had become to bring a healthy child into the world.

While this was a good goal to have, it was short in its overall purpose. Once my son was safely delivered, I was back on the smoking bandwagon within months. It was only once I decided to adapt this goal and make it relevant to me being healthy for the rest of my life that stopping smoking became a habit.

While motivation is the most important component of any goal-setting (and achieving) programme, there are techniques that can enhance your success. The good news is that you can learn how to use these techniques.

> 'A dream is just a dream. A goal is a
> dream with a plan and a deadline.'
>
> ---
>
> **HARVEY MACKAY**

There are many studies which depict people as having preferences when it comes to learning or being. I would like to highlight the word 'preferences' here. Some of us may be more auditory, visual, or kinaesthetic (atuned to feelings), but we can all use tools and techniques that are not in our preferred category and be successful.

Let's take your goal again. When you think of your goal, do you have a picture? For some, a picture can have sounds, smells and tasks attached to it. When you think of your goal, make the image so strong that you can feel it in your bones. It's your passion, your deepest desire.

Think about what that goal will do for you. What does it look, feel, sound like? The more specific you can be, the more emotions will be involved. Close your eyes. Can you see it? Maybe it has a smell. Hopefully you will feel a sensation in your body. Whereabouts is that feeling? Notice its intensity.

Spend some time visualising your goal every morning and evening. Bring it to life in your unconscious. Reset your brain from the clutter of your busy day-to-day. All your senses must be activated. See the colours. Hear the sounds.

Visualisation is about images, and for some of us, visualisation techniques will be extremely powerful. Maybe you have pictures of your dream house. Put them up where you can see them. Perhaps put them on a mood board and keep coming back with new pictures to add. Displays are excellent tools to enhance your goals as they are constant reminders.

For others, auditory techniques are more powerful. Can you hear the crowds cheering and clapping as you reach the finishing line of your first marathon? Your first born talking positively about you in front of his classmates?

Interestingly enough, when I think of how I used to procrastinate, I automatically have a song playing in my mind to remind me to get up, get rid of that clutter within me, and move towards motivation. When the music that we danced our first wedding dance to plays in the background, my husband and I will share a special look, even if we have had a difficult day. We are creatures of habit; we live life through our senses. Now is the time to use those senses to make what we want so enticing that nothing can stop us. The purpose, the goal will become part of our everyday life.

The good news is that we have already covered some of this in the first chapter. When you visualise your goal, you create a detailed ideal scenario – a blueprint of what you want. This tells your brain, your unconscious mind, and every cell of your body what it is that you want and can achieve. If the picture of the goal is compelling enough, the map to get there will be inside you somewhere.

One of the main reasons why people fail to accomplish their goal is fear. Fear is one of the deepest and most powerful emotions, and combatting it can lead to real struggles. In their mind, fearful people feel uncertain. Perhaps they are worrying about the steps which will lead to the goal. However, if they visualise the end result of their goal in their mind, it helps to make them more comfortable and fearless.

In a couple of months, I will be speaking on stage in front of hundreds of people. Instead of focusing on what could go wrong – and so much could go wrong at this point – I am choosing to focus on how I will be feeling once I have successfully completed the talk. I can hear my team congratulating me, I can feel the rush of adrenaline pumping through my veins, my heart swelling with pride and joy. Do I feel nervous about the event? All of the nervousness has turned to excitement. I cannot wait to stand up and share my story with my audience on the day.

Visualising my success is a simple way of reframing the event and reprogramming myself to enjoy the experience rather than letting myself be hijacked by feelings of fear and anxiety.

How to visualise

Imaginative visualisation is the reprogramming of your unconscious mind. Before you can achieve any goal, you must be able to see it clearly in your mind. Whatever image you are holding in your unconscious mind will happen more quickly in your life, so if you have previously struggled to accomplish your goals, you can now incorporate visualisation into the mix.

While visualisation can alter your unconscious mind and bring about lasting changes, not everyone knows how to visualise. How well do you visualise? How vivid are the images in your mind?

How we perceive something has a deep impact on our behaviour. For example, have you ever looked at buying a shirt on eBay? The way that the shirt is advertised will have a deep impact on your decision whether to buy it or not. There are websites that will let you download videos of people wearing the item so you can see for yourself how it flows when the body moves. This will contribute highly to my buying decision strategy as I am a deeply visual individual. For some people, their decision will be based on the description of the shirt; for others, it will be how the shirt feels (in which case, a website will not be their best shopping option). We act upon our perception of the world.

For some of us, after a while, self-doubt may come into play. But if you can imagine your goal, experience it as if it were real, then your neurology already knows what the outcome is like and how to get there. It's as simple as trusting yourself and the process.

> *'Impossible is nothing.'*
> ─────────
> **MUHAMMAD ALI**

Another internal visualisation tool is your auditory sense. Listen to your internal talk and use it to your advantage. Change the words you habitually use.

The relationship between thoughts and words is not one way. Thoughts may lead words, but words lead thoughts, too. This means that changing your words will change the way you experience life, immediately.

The way I speak to the people close to me, the words that I use, will have a significant impact on how they respond. For example, when my son cries because he doesn't want to go to school as it is swimming day, I help him to focus on what he wants to do at school instead. Then we can work on the fact that he will have to go swimming.

Focus more on what you want and less on what you don't want.

One simple way of changing your vocabulary to work for you is to break out of the prison of 'but' thinking. When you say, 'I would like to work on my goals, but I am so busy', what are you revealing about how you see your world? You are clearly indicating that you believe you have the choice to work on your goals, but the day to day will always have priority.

How can you get yourself to think outside the mould of this thinking? If you listen for it, you'll hear it all the time. I personally find that journaling or meditating while increasing awareness is incredibly powerful. It is fascinating to hold conversations with yourself and let your gut respond. Often in coaching contexts, I will ask my clients to say the first response that comes to mind, even if it does not make sense initially. Let the internal you speak rather than the conscious you.

The first time you go through this exercise, you may struggle to come up with a word or something meaningful. This is absolutely fine. Give yourself the luxury of time and patience, and trust in the process.

Here's an example of a 'but' conversation.

'I would like to get a job I enjoy, *but* I need to pay the mortgage.' That is interesting. Can I not get a job that I would enjoy and still pay the mortgage?

Now I would go deeper into this. What sort of job would be more enjoyable to me? What are the must haves? I would write down a list, comparing and contrasting what I have now with what I am missing.

Years ago, when I did a similar exercise, I found myself coming up with one compelling outcome – I needed less stress. I was in a corporate environment that promised a bright future and career advancement, and I thought that was what I wanted. After a deep discussion with myself, I realised that although it seemed to be a dream job, it was simply not part of my dream life.

It took a while and many lessons for me to move away from this environment. Focusing on what I wanted slowly drove me to where I am today. I still experience stress – don't we all? – but overall I am a million times more fulfilled in my professional and personal life than I ever dreamed I could be.

It is fascinating to listen to our inner talk. We are all conflicted in so many ways. All we need to do to underpin these conflicts is listen. We are all smart enough to make significant changes within our being, as long as they go alongside our flow (which is the focus of Week Five). Delving into the world of our intuition is helpful. It may take a while to develop, but the rewards of using intuition are plentiful, as we will observe later.

For example, in business, I often hear, 'I knew it! From the interview stage, I knew this individual was not the right person for the job.'

'So why did you hire them?' will always be my question. Even in business, an intuitive streak will support us in many situations.

Sometimes simply asking an empowering question can begin to unlock the prison door of limited thinking. For example:

- How can you work on your goals and be a great parent?

- How can you lose weight and take care of yourself?

- How can you leave him/her and enjoy being on your own?

Can you remember a time when you were happy? Tell yourself more about that.

Submodalities

Now that we've looked at imaginative visualisation and internal dialogue, let's delve deeper into our internal representations – our pictures, feelings, sounds which tap into our memories. And remember, all of this works alongside the unconscious mind.

Submodalities are the small adjustments we make to define what we hear, see, feel, taste, smell etc., and are a key part of what we train in NLP. For example, if I ask you to imagine a blue tree, your blue tree will almost certainly be different to the one I have in mind. It may be a deeper shade of blue, you may be able to feel the bark under your palms, or smell its sap. You may hear the sound of the leaves in the wind, and so on.

Using submodalities, we can enhance what we want.

EXERCISE 12

Imagine that you are standing in front of a mirror. In that mirror, you are seeing the future you – the you who has achieved exactly what your heart holds dear. Where are you? What are you wearing? What are you telling yourself? Enjoy what you are seeing. Notice the subtleties of the picture.

Now let's tweak it slightly and adjust its submodalities. I want you to make the picture brighter and more colourful. If there are sounds, make them louder; if there are twelve people cheering, make it 120, and so on. Find the details that will make you smile on the inside when you're looking at that picture.

Now, step into the mirror and let the picture become you. Feel the feelings of having achieved your goal. Notice where they are in your body, then make those feelings even stronger. Once you feel that you are full of those feelings, step out of the mirror.

Do this exercise at least a couple of times a day until it becomes super easy to wear that picture of you having achieved your goals.

Life is a mirror

I go into dark places sometimes. I can feel angry, sad, jealous, vengeful and so on. These feelings are natural and healthy – for a while. Grieving the death of a close friend for several weeks, for example, is completely healthy. We must go through these feelings in order to advance. It's getting stuck in negative scenarios which will cause us harm, especially when it comes to advancing our goals.

It is not easy to get out of negative thinking/feeling. I would encourage one step at a time, one success, one decision after another, while maintaining faith in yourself. Instead of looking outside yourself, blaming others for your problems, analyse your own challenges. Figure out what you need to learn or have already learned. Forgive, forget, and then move on.

The person you need to know more than anyone in your life is yourself. Take responsibility for your feelings – 'I am sad because I have lost a dear friend, and it is normal for me to feel this way. I will work on healing myself every day and accepting that particular loss.'

Each child within a family is different, even if they are all raised by the same parents. That is because everyone has their own destiny and lessons to learn for growth. Each person you meet will bring out different parts of you. Take time to be aware of this, and you will see it for yourself.

Write down what various relationships do for you. What do you get out of them?

If a woman believes all men are cheaters, she may well only attract men who cheat. If a man thinks all women are immature, he may well attract immature women. This is commonly known as the Law of Attraction.

> *'Think of the outer environment as a mirror of your inner environment. When you see something on the outside, such as an event or situation, look inside yourself for the reflection, the parallel, the connection.'*
>
> ———————
>
> **CHARLENE BELITZ AND MEG LUNDSTROM**

When someone comes into your life, step back and see that person for who they are and what they bring. This can be any person, not just a love relationship.

If you don't like what you see, ask yourself, 'What is it about me that needs to change?' Then you can internally thank the person for the learning and move on. I have several examples of having met people I simply detested. It was only once I realised what facet of me they were representing that I was finally able to let go of the hurt they caused.

Life is a string of key lessons that we can choose to learn from. The lessons we do not learn are the ones which repeat themselves. I recently wrote a blog about how it took me three burnouts to realise what I truly wanted in life. This is part of my personal journey which led me to write this book and share it with you.

If you understand this concept, then it makes absolute sense for you to think empowering thoughts. Think about how you will enhance yourself, your life, and ultimately the world. It relates to your awareness. Just because you are not aware of something doesn't mean that it does not exist. A lot in life is about thoughts and feelings. In a certain way, people you interact with are a projection of you. Be your mirror. What you don't like in others is what you don't like in yourself. The hardest person to see is yourself.

One of the things I struggled with most in my early adult years was how easy it is for people to manipulate others. Some would use emotional appeals so others would do exactly what they wanted. To me, they were using other people's goodwill to their own benefit.

Then I realised that was exactly how I behaved myself. Unconsciously, I would be a victim so that others would find me interesting; I would serve others so they would find me warm or welcoming; I would be clever so that everyone would want to be my friend. Manipulation is just a means of communication which is rather more convoluted than simply expressing what you want.

Recognising that manipulative streak in me generated a heap of energy which I can use on other aspects of my life. I am no longer playing games with others. I am clear, honest and authentic, which are qualities I admire in others also.

When you start to change, people will change the way they interact with you. It is that simple. Through the Law of Attraction, once you heal and know yourself, you attract new people into your life.

Let's take a hard look at ourselves. Complete the following statements:

- Other people love me because...

- My family loves me because...

- I love myself because...

If you want to be happy, thank the people who have challenged you for teaching you what you need to change about yourself. All you need is to be aware of these truths. Can you imagine how wonderful our world would be if everyone knew this and made their own necessary changes?

Everything starts with self. Are you ready to have a better life? The choice is yours.

Self-reflection

> *'Why are you so wary of thought?'* said the philosopher. *'Thought is the one tool we have for organizing the world.'*
>
> *'True. But thought can organize the world so well that you are no longer able to see it.'*
>
> ——————
>
> **ANTHONY DE MELLO**

People consider their problems to come from outside conditions. They try to change their surroundings in the vain hope things will improve. This seldom works because their thoughts are out of alignment.

> *'We don't see the world as it is, we see it as we are.'*
>
> ——————
>
> **ANAIS NIN**

Some people will claim life is wonderful and will attract pleasant experiences as a result. They are not Pollyanna-ish; they have chosen happiness over adversity. I still have a couple of skeletons in my closet, but they will not stop me from being happy and grateful for all that I have today. Those skeletons form part of the story that makes me the strong woman I am today.

Your predominant beliefs dictate your reality. You are continually shaping the world around you as a result of conscious and unconscious thoughts. Realise how much power, how much control over your own destiny you have.

> *Since our experience of life is really an experience of thought, the more we have on our mind, the more complicated everything seems, and the more the aperture of our consciousness tends to contract. Before we know it, all we can see when we look out into the world is our own thinking reflected back to us in the fun-house mirror of our own self-consciousness.'*
>
> ---
>
> **MICHAEL NEILL**

Mindfulness and quiet meditation will help you take the deep inner breath you need to grow. You do not need to be a yogi, follow a guru or light candles; all you need is to stop for a while and be conscious of your unconscious, your inner visualisations and thoughts, and how submodalities present themselves to you. All while remaining conscious of the thoughts in your mind, your feelings and the sensations around you.

> *'We cannot solve our problems with the same thinking we used when we created them.'*
>
> ───────
>
> **ALBERT EINSTEIN**

It makes sense to examine your thoughts to improve your conditions.

Free will or free choice?

Some people hold with the notion of free will. I am of the opinion that free will is an illusion. It is actually our unconscious beliefs reflected back at us in the guise of choices.

Millions of people have overcome limiting beliefs to create empowering lives. Life is a sequence of outcomes, symbols and shadows. Good or bad moments do not exist. Reality provides you with feedback to help you create new circumstances based on a shift in awareness.

Personal development and self-improvement lead you towards lasting change, if you are prepared to do the inner work. Obstacles reveal your path, so you end up working with them rather than avoiding them. You are the master of your own fate. Should you resign yourself to being a victim, life will offer you evidence that you are exactly that. Freedom of choice means life is neutral and ready to respond to your thoughts.

> *'Life proceeds out of your intentions for it. This is the fuel that drives the engine of creation in your life.'*
>
> **NEALE DONALD WALSCH**

Negative thoughts contain lessons to enhance your personal evolution and create a new reality. The cynic finds this unwelcome, but the optimist recognises it as an opportunity to correct their thoughts. If you experience chaos and confusion inside your mind, your external world reflects that. You see what you believe because you are the interpreter of everything. If you're chaotic, what you'll hear and see is chaos. If you do not examine your thoughts, they will become habitual and are bound to show up in your reality sooner or later.

Some days, everything seems to go wrong. It begins with one bad event – the car won't start; the alarm didn't go off – that affects our state of mind. That leads to another bad event, and then another, and before we know it, the world looks like an ugly place. Put enough of those days together and life can become almost unbearable. Yet, nothing in the world creates our misery. It is our response, our own state of consciousness that creates the ugliness.

No matter what happens, look for the good and you'll find it. When life takes a bite at you, simply stop, breathe, and take back control by placing yourself at the helm of what happens next. A positive thinker does not refuse to recognise the negative; they refuse to dwell on it. Positive thinking is a form of thought which habitually looks for the best results from the worst conditions.

It is much easier to eliminate hatred from within you than from the rest of the world. And the key to banishing something from your external world is to eliminate it from your internal world. Accept that hate is a product of thought and has no true value in your world. If you accept hate, your reality mirror – your perceived external world – will change to reflect that new perspective. The external hatred that you see will be replaced by its opposite, love.

I understand that this takes practice. It starts with being aware of what goes on internally, catching yourself having a negative moment.

Here was my challenge today. After having spent another night awake looking after my small daughter, I was asked by my husband whether I would 'just' take care of the laundry. Oh, how I got annoyed with this request, when in fact, the laundry took me five minutes to handle. I caught my feelings just in time, before they could override my system or colour my judgement. It was like looking into my reality mirror and seeing anger, then choosing whether or not to release it or to do something else.

For the next week, express and feel happiness. Fake it until you believe it. In one week's time, notice your external reality. If you do it correctly, you will notice an increase in your perceived external happiness. People will seem more cheerful as compared to the previous week, and that is due to the minor change in your inner state.

A continuation of this practice will eliminate much of the sadness from your reality. It is time to break any negative thought spirals. You are in control. Make that promise to yourself, and write it down.

If your reality mirror reflects many broken relationships back at you, then you are probably not having a good relationship with yourself. If you dislike yourself to an unhealthy level, your reality mirror will reflect people disliking themselves. If all you experience in your reality mirror are people who are too self loving, then you are likely guilty of the same practice.

Use your reality mirror to see what you like and dislike about your external reality. Then, look inward to see where those aspects reside within you. The ones you like, you keep. The ones you dislike, you discard. The ones you desire, you add.

Timeline overview

We talked in Week Three about setting up a step-by-step milestone approach to reaching your goals. Once it is set, let it go. Let yourself flow and live life in the present, and your unconscious will help you towards achieving your milestones. The last thing you want to do is create frustration and stress.

EXERCISE 13

Here's a little exercise that I run in practically all of my training sessions. If I was to ask you where, in the space around you, you would place your last birthday, where would you be pointing? Take the first answer that comes to mind. Now if I was to ask you where you would place your next birthday, where would you point?

All events in our lives trace what we call a timeline. From birth to our future goals, everything is organised in a certain way. For some it may run through us, for others in front of us. Sit and imagine your timeline. Close your eyes and float above your body, so high that you can see your whole timeline as a little line or squiggle.

Now see the place in your future where you will achieve your goal and float into that place. Supercharge that event and notice everything around you. Enjoy it.

Once you have done that, turn around. From that place in the future, look towards today. Notice all the events that need to happen to make your goal become reality. This will give you the key to success.

Run this exercise as often as you want.

You can can download a Preferred Representational System test from our website (http://verytraining.co.uk/representation/). This will help you identify which sense you prefer to perceive information through. Pay attention to stimulation of that specific sense. For example, if you prefer to percieve information through touch, when you wash the dishes, pay attention to the feel of the hot water and the bubbles. It's a rather soothing exercise to accompany mundane activities which tend to be muted. Unmute the unconscious mind while paying less attention to the conscious mind.

Persistence

Be unreasonable about the achievement of your goals. You need to get comfortable with being crazy, ridiculous, unrealistic, and relentless. Like a child learning to walk, fall down and stand up once more. And when you get there, give yourself the biggest smile.

Persistence is not about pursuing your goals when everything is going well; it's about pursuing your goals even when you're getting little to no results and you feel like you're wasting your time. The minute you decide to give up, your dreams, goals and aspirations will become history. If there is one trait that you must have in order to be successful, it is persistence. It doesn't matter how long it takes to achieve your goals, it is all worth it.

If you do feel like giving up, then it is time to take a step back and reflect on what it is that you want, define your true purpose, and reconnect with who you are.

Week Five

Flow

This week, we will be focusing on a concept called flow. Flow is pivotal to making everything easy and effortless. After all, we live in the here and now, so at some point our wishes for the future need to be incorporated seamlessly into our daily living.

There is obviously a lot to be said for living in the present moment and consciously bringing our awareness to that. The challenge is being in the present while observing the potential of the future. Flow brings the concept of the future self into the present, making it easier to move towards what we want.

Achieving flow requires you to:

- Choose work you love

- Choose an important task, making sure it's challenging, but not too hard

- Find your peak quiet time

- Clear away distractions

- Learn to focus

- Enjoy yourself

- Keep practising

- Choose work you love

'You've got to find what you love. And that is as true for your work as it is for your lovers. Your work is going to fill a large part of your life, and the only way to be truly satisfied is to do what you believe is great work. And the only way to do great work is to love what you do.'

STEVE JOBS

Think about your hobbies and interests. What do you enjoy? Put some time into finding out what it is about the activity that makes you love it. What feelings does it evoke in you? When have you been the most proud of yourself? What had you achieved then?

Now do a little research. What do your hobbies and interests have that might be in a job description? For example, searching the internet or solving puzzles are examples of looking for answers. These skills could be used in a career in research. Are you someone people ask for advice? Maybe putting the pieces together and looking for the right answer are natural skills you have which could lead to several career options.

My French acquaintance, Florence, took the courageous step to quit the world of civil engineering and choose a career that flows easily and gracefully with her life. That required some sacrifices, but to this day, she has no regrets.

It makes my blood boil when I hear we should be doing what we love to do all the time without any step-by-step advice on how to find what it is we love to do. I remember job counsellors at school telling me to opt for this or that option, and undergoing tests which told me which career was more suited for me, but the important question is not, 'What do I want to do?' It's more about, 'Who am I and what is my purpose?'

In my line of work, I often meet individuals who persist in working in jobs they hate, because they rely on that sole source of income. They drift aimlessly through life, leading 'lives of quiet desperation' as Henry David Thoreau so eloquently put it. I've often wondered what the purpose is behind this and have come up with two assumptions.

Assumption #1: They don't know what they love to do and have never really thought about it.

Assumption #2: Fear. Fear of not being able to uphold their lifestyle; fear of no steady source of income; fear of what other people may think or say about them; etc.

That old friend fear again, one of the hardest emotions to overcome, and I can completely relate to that. However, if we conquer the indecision in assumption #1 and act, we will likely conquer the fear in assumption #2.

If you uncover the destination you want to steer your life towards then day-to-day decisions become easier. All uncertainty and burdens will be lifted from your shoulders and the journey will be truly joyful. By the time you have finished reading this book, I trust you will be experiencing that joy.

When I started thinking about what I would love to do, initially, I wanted to leave everything and run, overwhelmed about the things I didn't want and still had in my life. I wanted to be free to live my life as I saw fit. Then I blended my new flowing beliefs into my day-to-day and trusted that the answer was already in me. I didn't have to drastically change my world to find my purpose. I just continued living and avoided procrastinating.

Trust in the process. Your brain has absorbed all sorts of information and experiences, and it has the answer ready to be unravelled.

I currently have a student in my mindfulness class who is struggling to do her homework. She openly told the group last week that the reason for her struggles was that she felt as though something big was going to come out. Something that she wasn't prepared to take on, so she was procrastinating. In my mind, this lady is very courageous to acknowledge this to herself (let alone the whole group) and is definitely on an amazing journey.

Who cares about the time it takes to come up with an answer, as long as it is the right one for you. It is fine to take some time on this point to reflect and be aware of what truly excites you.

Go back and think of your accomplishments as a child. What kind of skills and interests revolved around your accomplishments? What did people praise you for doing? What did your teachers or parents say you had a skill or knack for?

Skills. You've got to leverage what you're strong at. Everybody has skills. By using your skills, you've got a head start.

Interests. You've got to love what you do. By including interests, you include another form of anti-quitting mechanism. Focus on generating as many skills and interests as you can possibly think of and write them all down. Writing things down allows you to make connections you've never thought of before because you see them on paper. It also allows you to free up room in your brain for other thoughts. Writing down sometimes helps you access a deeper level of your unconscious.

You may find that your skills and interests are gravitating in the same direction. As a child, I loved Lego. It was a way of going into my own world – a form of deep meditation. And I loved building and creating things – two amazing skills to have.

Set some private time with no distractions. Then ask yourself a clear question, and write the answer down. What is the question you should ask yourself?

'What do I love to do?'

That question is a bit broad, so let's narrow it down a little. Try asking yourself, 'What would I love to do on a daily basis utilising both my skills and my interests that will add significant value to people?' The more detailed and clear the question, the easier it will be to answer it. The 'add value' part will lead you to find a way to flow in the world doing what you love. You will automatically filter out all the common answers that people come up with when asked what they love to do, for example, 'I love to watch TV', or 'I love to play video games'.

Many people make the mistake of focusing on how to make money. Money is just a by-product of adding value for people in the form of a product or service. If you choose to set up your own business, reflect on the value you bring to others instead of how much money you can make.

Open up Word or take a blank sheet of paper and write that question at the top. Here it is again:

'What would I love to do on a daily basis utilising both my skills and my interests that will add significant value to people?'

Looking at your list of skills and interests, write a list of answers to this question. Just write. The answers don't have to be perfect or even make sense, because sooner or later, you will connect the dots.

Here's a story to illustrate what I'm talking about. A small town with a ski resort attracted a lot of tourists, which helped the town's economy. However, when it snowed, the snowfall collected on the power cables until the weight was enough to collapse the cables, resulting in several power outages. Slowly but surely, the tourists stopped coming.

The townspeople held a meeting to discuss how to solve the problem. Solutions were tossed around for quite some time, until somebody shouted, 'Let's hang pots of honey on the power cables to make the bears climb up. Their movement will shake the snow off.'

Deciding to play along, someone else said, 'How will we refill the pots of honey?'

'We'll use a helicopter,' a third person replied.

Then the answer dawned upon them. If a helicopter flew by the power lines, the wind from the propellers would shake the snow off.

Don't disregard any answers, no matter how ridiculous they may seem, because more often than not, they lead to results. It's all part of the process. Remember my first response to this question was to recall how much I enjoyed playing with Lego. Write until you have twenty answers and look them over. This will inspire you to think of new, creative answers that you would not have come up with before.

Choose an important task

Now the time comes for focus. If you try to do a bunch of things at once, nothing will get done. By focusing all your power, energy, time, thinking, etc. on one goal, you can accomplish it quickly and effectively.

Imagine you're a cheetah and you see two juicy gazelles grazing in the grass. Spending your time chasing both = no food = death. It may take time to hunt one down and catch it, but when you do, you'll be recharged. You will also collect information on how the gazelles run, which direction they run, where they like to graze, etc., which will help you catch more gazelles in the future.

> *'The world is changed by your example, not your opinion.'*
>
> ———
>
> **PAULO COELHO**

Focus on one thing and do it well. You deserve it. Look over your list and choose one idea that is the most appealing to you. You may find you can combine a few ideas into one idea. You may want to zero in on the ideas that combine your skills and interests. Choose one idea that holds the greatest value not just for you, but for other people. Then invest in yourself and make it happen.

The challenge of daily life is to complete a variety of tasks at the right time, which can be difficult. This challenge is made easier if you learn to perform the right task at the right time. The first step is to make a list of the tasks you need to complete in a day and write them down on a piece of paper.

Then categorise your tasks according to whether each one is interesting or boring for you. For example, data typing may seem a bit boring, while learning something new is quite interesting.

It's now time to relate the nature of the job to your emotional state. Look at your list of tasks to be completed in a day, remembering that the interesting tasks require less time than the boring tasks. To perform the right task at the right time, just analyse your mood and act according to it. The most effective time to learn something is when you are feeling curious. Work which requires creativity and an analytical mind should be done when you are feeling excited, because excitement will help you to think in an analytical way. Mundane tasks that don't require much concentration can be completed when you're feeling bored or tired.

When running through this exercise, you may find that certain times of day are more auspicious than others for performing specific tasks. Write down and work with your trends. Are you more inclined to do some strategic thinking in the morning or the afternoon? I have set Fridays as my admin days, and Wednesdays are my creative days, specifically Wednesday mornings.

When it comes to completing tasks in the most effective way, you need to know how to prioritise them. The best time managers in the world know that they don't have the authority and the power to perform everything, so they select the tasks that they have to accomplish – those that are crucial to the operation and maintenance of the business, considering the time and financial constraints.

Keep in mind, though, that task prioritisation has opportunity costs. If you choose a particular task at a particular time, you are rejecting all of the other tasks that you could have accomplished at that particular time. To make sure that you can actually complete the job, you have to be the one who does the choosing. Do not simply go with the flow or allow others to determine the tasks for you.

There's no way that you can guess the right number of hours you'll need to accomplish all of the tasks at hand. If you learn to focus on the tasks that matter the most, you can make the most of your time. Also, plan some downtime. Leisure time is extremely important for our health.

Here are the traditional methods to improve your task prioritisation:

Create your own list. It's critical that you create your own list of jobs and actually write them down. You can write your list on a sheet of paper, in a notebook, or on your mobile device or desk computer – whatever works best for you. This way, you won't miss out any task.

When you're listing your jobs, don't think too much about prioritising them. Your main goal here is to identify all of your tasks. Avoid making too many to-do lists.

One tip that has helped me survive the endless refilling of task lists is to review the list at the end of each day, once my work is finished. I cross out what I've achieved and write down what I need to accomplish the next day. Once this task is complete, my time is mine as I can stop overthinking my list.

Determine the due dates of each task. It's better to base your due date on the time the task is required and not when you can actually perform it.

A calendar or diary is a great tool to use when you're setting deadlines. It helps you to be clear on how you will accomplish something when you can physically see what steps you need to accomplish and by when. I also like to keep a mood board in my diary. Being highly visual, I find this helps my motivation and spirit to move forward.

Make sure your tasks are challenging, but not too hard. Getting into the flow is one of the most powerful ways of achieving big, audacious goals. Flow is the secret to high performance as it'll open doors for you to create a more satisfying, more fulfilling and happier life. It doesn't matter whether you are a world-class athlete, a corporate CEO, a college professor, a martial arts trainer or a chess player, you can always use the flow state to enhance your performance and achieve what you want.

Flow is also a positive mental state that will enhance your health and well-being by reducing stress and boosting your immune system. The question is, what do you actually need in order to get into the flow state? You need a challenge. Perhaps one of achieving what you want in seven weeks...

Things that are too easy won't get you into flow. Nor will extreme difficulty get you there, so design an optimal challenge for yourself. Plan tasks that are worthwhile (for yourself), ambitiously achievable, and with a nice challenge throughout the process so you have to work for it. To attain flow state and enjoy its immense benefits, strike a balance between the challenge and your current skills level. If there is too little challenge, then boredom will set in and your motivation will lessen. On the other hand, too much challenge will result in self-doubt, anxiety and stress. Negative emotions will block flow.

The flow state is one of total absorption, where you take massive actions without any thoughts of yourself or time. This is why sports people, artists, actors and writers use the flow state to improve their performance and achieve new career heights.

Now it is time to pull out your list of goals. Is there anything you can cross off today because it is not necessary any more? Probably not. The long-standing items on my list are usually large, time-consuming projects or difficult tasks that I am unsure how to complete. Some items are vague drafts linked to my end destination – I have an idea of what these are and am still working on them. Others, like getting the builder to provide a quote to change my front door, simply require me to pick up the phone. Those sort of goals are easy to cross off my list right now.

It is rewarding to cross several items off your list during the course of a day. Ask yourself why each item is on your list. Will it make your life easier? Will it increase sales? Will it make you happier? Pick something (anything) and just do it. If you need help, ask for it. You are likely to know someone who has experience in your chosen task. Ask them for help, or model yourself on them. In most cases, they will be able to give you good advice, but in some cases, they may be glad to do the task for you. You may even learn that they could use your help with something, too.

Building a business network or mastermind group is the best way to get help with difficult tasks. Interacting and working with colleagues will help you to see your own strengths and accomplish your goals more effectively using all the resources available to you. For example, I work with an amazing assistant, Sam. She has been instrumental in building my business and alongside me every step of the way. If I know that something will take me ages to perform, such as updating my website or posting a blog, I will ask for her help. It takes me a week to do what she can do in an hour, which frees me up to write blogs, research content, coach or train students and clients. Where I can add value to my life and the lives of others, I will never hesitate to choose that.

Find your peak quiet time

Quiet time provides an opportunity for us to be still and enjoy our own company. Most people are busy beating the traffic, running errands, cleaning, shopping, and attending events they never planned for. You can break out of this cycle by adding quiet time and balancing the act.

Here are some things you can do to ensure that you get some quality time for yourself:

- Remove all distractions – turn off the TV, phone, etc.

- Sit in a quiet spot and become mindful of your breathing, contemplating your inhaling and exhaling

- Enjoy your own company

- If you find your mind wandering, gently bring it back to your breathing

Once you're more practised in the skill of mindfulness or meditation, you will be able to do it anywhere and at any time. Develop this habit and let others know how much you value your time-out period. Before you know it, you'll be feeling finer than frog's hair.

Let's get started with some simple steps.

Schedule. Establish the amount of time you will spend on quiet contemplation per day, allowing more room for your project after that time. You may want to use a planner, an electronic calendar such as Google Calendar or Microsoft Office Outlook, or Team Week works well for up to five persons. When you schedule your time, be specific and make sure you add enough time for each activity. Take into consideration any obstacles and things that you need to experience your quiet time each day.

Be committed. Stick to the daily quiet time you set. Make it your first priority in your schedule. You have to be determined to make the lifestyle changes necessary to achieve your goal of having quiet time. Be consistent and persistent.

Consider morning or night. Most people find first thing in the morning or last thing at night the best times for their quiet time.

Limit distractions. Avoid the television at all costs during your quiet time. Create a serene environment that will increase harmony and tranquility, and don't allow anyone to intrude into your environment once you have set your special time aside. I have set my own space in my home that will always be ready for my individual practice.

Keep a journal. Write down your experiences during your silent moments to capture the benefits of starting this journey. You will soon see that it is relevant for your life. You will also be able to reflect back on the lessons you have learned along the way.

Don't stop. If you miss your special time one day, start again the next day. Keep on keeping on. When you become proficient at it, you will feel that you have missed something important if you stop.

Balance your daily activities and focus on your goals if you want to be successful. It will improve your lifestyle dramatically.

Clear away distractions

A distraction is anything that comes between you and your goals. If it doesn't take you closer to your goal, then it's dragging you away.

When you're working alone, it's easy to think that a couple of minutes to make a quick call or open some mail won't make a difference. Then one thing leads to another and you end up far from where you wanted to be after an hour has flown by. I learned that giving in to distractions is a choice as I become conscious of the little things that I allowed to take me away from my task.

For example, if I had let myself be run by the endless responsibilities of daily life, then I would never have written this book. My book-writing time was precious to me, so once I had set it, I allowed no distractions until either I had run out of ideas or my planned time was up.

The same is true when I spend time with my children. I will be 100% present or not there at all. It is a choice.

The only way to manage potential distractions is to control two things: your environment and your actions. You can choose to eliminate distractions by creating a work environment that helps you to focus and shields you from distractions. Then choose to master your work habits. Do you tend to multi-task? If that's the case, set a timer to help you stay focused on one task until it's complete. Then reward yourself and set it again. You can accomplish an amazing amount in two fifty-minute sessions of focused, productive work.

If you want to boost your productivity, learn how to concentrate and avoid distractions. Here are tips on how to cut out distractions so you can focus more:

Structure your environment. The place where you work or study can have a great impact on your ability to concentrate. Locate yourself away from clutter. If you are working online, close all browsers on your computer apart from the one you are working on. If you are having family time, put your phone down. If you want to learn something new, focus on what you are being taught. Your shopping list can wait.

Clarify your objectives. By setting clear objectives, you will be able to concentrate more. If you are not sure what the end result will be, uncertainty will make it impossible for you to focus and you will be easily distracted.

Take regular breaks. Regular breaks help improve your alertness and concentration levels. Long studying or working hours not only affect your performance and mental capacity, but your physical health, too. Taking regular breaks when studying or working prevents tense muscles and eye strain.

Routine. Set yourself a time frame within which you will study or work, then stick to it. If you need time for fitness classes, dog walks, collecting your children from school, cleaning your house, etc., that's OK as long as you include them in your daily routine before they become distractions.

Keep refreshments handy. Thirst and hunger can be major distractions when you are working or studying. Have plenty of healthy snacks (such as fruit, cheese, healthy snack bars or peanut butter) and water near your study or work space so that you can stay energised and hydrated without being distracted.

Communicate. Tell the members of your family or your colleagues when you will be busy working so they can save any questions for when you've finished. You can also put a note on your door asking not to be disturbed.

Learn to focus

Have you ever had trouble finishing something that you started? You're not alone. We are all bombarded with information, which can be conflicting, and are often under pressure to portray a perfect life. No wonder so many of us are lost.

If you have tasks or projects that you have not finished or have lost interest in, you have a lack of focus. It can make you feel like a failure when you don't seem to be able to accomplish anything meaningful, but this is not the truth. If you learn to focus properly, you will be able to become successful at anything you do. It is a skill you can learn.

Why is focus so important? Focus helps you to:

- Set clear objectives

- Take action

- Identify specific and productive steps to take

- Keep track of your progress

- Avoid distractions

- Work efficiently

There are two types of focus. I call them big picture (broad) focus and action steps (narrow) focus. Big picture focus means you're looking at the vision, dream, goal or project from a distance, allowing you to gain a clear idea of what you want to achieve and the best way to make it happen. Action steps focus means taking one thing at a time. Once you are clear on your big picture and have assessed the challenges, possibilities and threats, narrow your focus to concentrate on the steps you need to take to bring your vision/dream/goal/project to fruition. Take one step at a time and only focus on that step.

It is crucial to have a clear and detailed plan of action. However, you can have the best plan in the world, but without you taking action, nothing will come to fruition. This is why I call the narrow focus 'action steps'.

What you focus on, you create in your life. So, it is critical that you focus on things that are worthwhile. The keys to creating focus are the following:

- Your commitment to your vision and the process (the action steps)

- Achievable, measureable and realistic goals/ steps

- Staying focused on the positive and paying attention to the benefits and gains of each action step

- Improving your focus by working at it every day

Also crucial are:

Enthusiasm. Without enthusiasm, you may not find the journey interesting enough to continue. When you first set your goal or vision, enthusiasm gives you the zest or oomph to tackle things head on. As time progresses, it is natural to lose some of the oomph. However, if you learn how to keep yourself enthused and recommit regularly to your goal or vision, you will be adding fuel to carry on. Positive self-talk helps you to stay in the oomph mode, so get excited about what you are working towards. With a positive attitude, nothing will ever seem hopeless or a waste of time. If you do encounter a setback, you will get right back up and move on.

Self-discipline. Focus takes tremendous self-discipline. You have to be strong enough to stick to your plan, track your progress, be receptive to changing it if necessary, and execute it daily. You have to be dedicated to avoiding temptations and self-doubt, but still be flexible if the unexpected happens.

Avoiding procrastination. Procrastination is like a thief stealing your results. If you tend to over think things, stop. You're doing yourself no favours and you will set yourself up for failure.

Consistency. Spending a set amount of time on your action steps brings your vision closer every day. It's like exercising for twenty minutes or brushing your teeth for three minutes per day. If you do it consistently and daily, it is not much of an effort and you will see the benefits. However, if you exercise once a week for 140 minutes or brush your teeth once a week for twenty-one minutes, you will not get fit and your breath will not smell great.

Tenacity. As the saying goes, 'Quitters never win and winners never quit'. Creating and keeping a strong focus is hard work, but it is a skill that will serve you for the rest of your life. Believe in yourself and your ability to succeed in whatever you do.

Enjoy yourself

What does it mean to have fun? What does it mean to have a good time? Have you done either lately?

Enjoyment is defined as a good or pleasing experience that comes from the use of something, and it is a personal thing. A spouse may enjoy the use of your credit card to purchase new shoes. The use of a cruise ship may give you pleasurable experiences while on holiday.

We often chase the job, the promotion, the pay rise without taking time to enjoy being with the people we come into contact with daily. We pass trees and flowers without thinking. Of course, I am aware of bills, mortgages and car maintenance. Life is muchmore enjoyable than that if you slow down and take time to enjoy the world around you.

Do you have a favourite song? Songs can uplift you and change your outlook on life. In 1992, Blind Melon released a song called 'Change' which absolutely changed the course of my life. It talks about reaching for the sun when things are not so great. It talks about being aware of all the things you can choose to change to get you out of the misery of daily life. I often play this oldie as it reminds me of my commitment to remaining positive no matter what.

Of course, I have some good days and some bad days. However, my good days tip the scales heavily, especially since I have chosen to enjoy myself. So how do you do that?

Plan a time that you are going to participate in an activity that you like. Imagine that you are watching your favourite sports team or on a cruise ship – whatever works for you – then write it down on paper. Good feelings will arise with the anticipation of making plans. After that, do it.

While you are enjoying yourself, feel the moment. Really experience it. Now this is living.

Many of us assume that we need to make drastic changes to our habits, routines and/or bank balances to be happy. In reality, that's not the case. Often, we already have everything we need to enjoy life – it's just a question of prioritising what's really important.

Here are fifteen simple ways you can enjoy your life more, starting today.

1. Focus on yourself. Other people will always be on hand to offer their opinions and advice. Ultimately, however, it's you, and you alone, who has to live with the consequences of your decisions.

2. Make time to relax and destress. Making time to reconnect with yourself leaves you better equipped to deal with challenging periods.

3. Avoid the media. It's all too easy to get sucked into public drama, online and offline. If something important happens, you'll know about it. Otherwise, ignore the the news, and save your energy and time for something more worthwhile.

4. Nurture your positive relationships with friends and family. Identify the people who lift you up and focus your energy on them.

5. Meet new people. Community is one of the most important needs we have. If you make a consistent effort to meet new people, you help yourself to fulfil that need and introduce yourself to new ideas and perspectives.

6. Explore new places. New places and cultures offer you a different perspective on the world and add a healthy dose of inspiration and possibility to your life.

7. Keep a wish list. Whenever you think of something you'd like to try, or a place you'd like to visit, write it down. It keeps the dream alive and stops it fizzling out as a forgotten thought.

8. Try new things. Commit to trying a certain number of items from your wish list each year to make sure they don't just stay as wishes.

9. Spend money on experiences, not possessions. It's experiences, not possessions, that create memories and meaning.

10. Cut down your junk. Physical clutter equals mental clutter. Reducing the amount of stuff around you fosters a calm mental state.

11. Make time for gratitude and appreciation.
    Write down three things you feel grateful for
    each day. This helps you focus more on what
    you're grateful for in life.

12. Track how you're spending your time. It's easy
    to get to the end of a day and wonder where
    all the time went, so track how you spend your
    time in an average week. When you're
    conscious of how you're spending your hours,
    you can make the most of the time you have
    on this planet.

13. Be deliberate in your choices. There have
    never been so many opportunities to create a
    lifestyle that you truly love. Be deliberate in
    your life choices. Remember that it's your life
    and no-one else's.

14. Invest in yourself. The more self-aware and
    self-accepting you are, the happier you will be.
    Make time to read personal development books,
    journal, and focus on being compassionate
    towards yourself.

15. Remember that all feelings pass. A key part
    of enjoying life is accepting that you're not
    going to feel 100% happy 100% of the time.
    During the more challenging times,
    remember that life is one big cycle of ups and
    downs.

Keep practising

This section is about practising. It is easy for me to tell you what to do, but you need to experience life, make mistakes, and enjoy yourself. Maintain a curious and non-judgemental attitude.

Now add some persistence to the mix. Napoleon Hill lists persistence as one of the essential steps towards riches in his book *Think and Grow Rich*.

> *'We are what we repeatedly do. Excellence, therefore, is not an act, but a habit.'*
>
> ———
>
> **ARISTOTLE**

Are you frustrated by your career success (or lack of it)? Are you really good at what you do but you can't get anyone to realise it? Do you find it difficult to be taken seriously? Do you wish you could find your dream job and just be happy?

There's nothing wrong with you. Most people have felt like you do at some point in their career. The good news is that a problem well stated is a problem half solved. It just takes a different way of doing things to create the different result that you are looking for. There's nothing to be afraid of. It all comes down to whether or not you believe that you are capable of learning something new. That's all. Start with something fun.

Flow is to be completely in tune with who you are and where you are going. This is what I imagine is going on when I watch tai chi masters practising their form, slow and controlled, soft and powerful, where every cell of the body follows its purpose alongside the mind's will. And this, I would agree, takes a lot of practise.

> *'You are in an ecstatic state to such a point that you feel as though you almost don't exist. I have experienced this time and time again. My hand seems devoid of myself, and I have nothing to do with what is happening. I just sit there watching it in a state of awe and wonderment. And [the music] just flows out of itself.'*
>
> **QUOTED BY DR MIHALY CSIKSZENTMIHALYI**

In order to function and be engaged in our day-to-day life, our mind needs to delete, distort and generalise information. Generally speaking, to take on a new task, our brain needs to switch off another function from our awareness and run that program in our unconscious mind. For example, it is rare for us to feel the sensation of wearing socks while we're driving.

Flow is having the capacity in our own neurology to become ultra aware of this. You may recall the moment where you met a loved one for the first time. You were utterly present, physically and mentally. Sounds, smells and images merged into one with the emotion running through you. As humans, we can have the joy of experiencing these moments by accident or through practice.

The route to achieving flow is setting goals, eliminating negative thoughts, beliefs and decisions, understanding our purpose and what our milestones are, focusing on what we want, and integrating our beings into a whole and complete unit.

Interestingly enough, the concept of flow came through a study of happiness led by Dr Csikszentmihalyi.

Once you live in happiness, as opposed to wishing and hoping for it, your world will always flow in the direction of your dreams. Your life will work in all areas. You were born knowing how to be happy; you did not learn it from your parents or friends. Somehow, though, that knowing may be buried so deeply that you may think you have lost it. The truth is that you have not; you have allowed negative emotions to cover your truth.

When you reject what others tell you about how life should be, you will remember what you knew when you arrived in this world as an innocent child. As a baby, you smiled and laughed and attracted warm hugs – adults reflecting their happiness by responding to yours. The secret to happiness is not a secret at all, just a memory. Feeling happy is all about your thoughts. You can't have a feeling without first having a thought. Therefore, if you're feeling happy, it's because you're thinking happy thoughts.

Have you ever had a tiny thought that just escalated? A little something that irked you until you were on the rampage? Then you opened your mouth and mean, hateful words spewed forth, sometimes directed at yourself. All because of a stray little thought that needed to be caught in its embryonic stage and allowed to die a gentle death. When you learn how to pay attention to your feelings, you can catch these bad mood makers.

It's not easy, paying attention to our feelings. We're so used to just being, we don't stop to analyse our thoughts. Why should we? Remember, though, that happy thoughts create happy feelings. And happy feelings create more happy thoughts. And more happy thoughts create happiness.

EXERCISE 14

Choose a specific activity linked to your goal – maybe one last push to reach a milestone. Before your begin that activity, pause. Take three deep breaths and concentrate on them. Enjoy complete silence and stillness within.

Become aware of the present moment as if it was the past, the present, and the future. Position yourself at the centre of time. Become aware of all the choices and decisions you have made as a sequence of events, and your future choices and decisions in their own sequence.

Begin your activity. Make it a meditative practice and intensify your focus. If you can, lead that activity in your peripheral vision. Expand your awarenesss while becoming super sensitive. Mute your conscious mind, quieten any chatter. If you do wander off into other thoughts or self-talk, gently redirect your awareness to the present.

Treat this activity as a sacred gift that brings you closer to achieving the goal(s) you have set for yourself.

The purpose of flow is to hit a higher level of integration between your today and your tomorrow, programming your mind and body to achieve just that. The experience of flow must be a pleasurable one. If it's not, I would encourage you to revisit Week Two and work some more on your limiting decisions and beliefs.

I often find myself juggling life and only having a few hours a week to myself. With that in mind, I have come up with my own strategies to practise flow and continue to develop myself. Some of my strategies are simple:

- Focus on one thing at a time

- Reward yourself

- Never put something off until tomorrow if it can be done today

- Plan your day/week

- Relish your relationships with others and yourself

- Be honest

- Value your mind as well as your body

- Practise meditation and/or tai chi

This list isn't exhaustive. Think of what daily practice strategies you can set for yourself to achieve your own flow. The biggest prize in all of this is living a completely fulfilling life.

Week Six

Learning To Trust Yourself

This week, I'm going to ask you to set aside your driving energy, your lists, your plans, and so on to work on your intuition. Basically, take your goals and completely forget about them – just for this week.

In order to have good intuitive qualities, you must first get to know yourself. My life today is mostly guided by my intuition, and the only time I find myself in a difficult situation is when I fail to heed its warnings.

When have you listened to your intuition and it has saved you from a whole lot of drama? When have you thought you were following your intuition, and it resulted in pain or suffering? Do you trust your intuition? How much? Before we delve further into the subject, write down your answers to these questions.

Intuition is a natural ability and an intellectual skill. It is actually a brain state that you can learn to tune into at will. The word intuition comes from the Latin word *intueor*, meaning to look at or in. It is described as a knowing that occurs without our knowing how or why.

Your intuition works simultaneously with the rest of your awareness. To be able to use it at will, you need to train your mind and become aware of your whole mental process. I am going to ask you lots of questions this week, so grab your journal and write down all the answers that come to mind, especially those that do not make sense at the moment. You may be surprised at what you learn. This process will also help you put together a picture of how your intuition works or doesn't work at this moment of your life.

What does the word intuition mean to you? How does your intuition make itself known to you? Is it a sound, a feeling, a smell, a taste? Is it a visual flash of insight, a dream, a gut sense of knowing? Where in your body do you get a sense of your intuition?

It's important to identify at least one time in your life where your intuition has influenced you. Have you ever had a hunch that turned out to be correct? It could be something as simple as the fact someone was going to phone you or come and visit. Stop for a moment and allow that memory to play through your mind. See it like a movie on your internal mind screen, or replay it like a CD. Relive the experience for a minute or two, then write it down in detail. Try to recall exactly what you felt or experienced.

Do you have trouble trusting your intuition? Be honest as your base point is essential in defining your future skill level. How do you decide if what you are sensing is intuition or fear-based anxiety? How do you know if it is intuition or just your thoughts? Most people in the early stages of developing intuition will not be able to differentiate between the two, and this is absolutely fine. This is the reason we begin with this first step – getting to know your intuition and journaling your experiences – so don't underestimate the value of this part of the process.

There are two types of intuition: intuition with precedent and intuition without precedent.

Intuition with precedent

Intuition with precedent is based upon sensations or feelings that we identify or label according to a known outcome. For example, if we have a sense of foreboding one morning and then experience something terrible, we will always associate that type of experience with that feeling. Intuition with precedent is understanding the here and now based upon past events. This type of intuition can only ever be 98% right at most as it is based on our own interpretation and awareness of our internal feelings, like an internal radar based on what is going on behind us.

The examples below are just two from thousands of people's accounts of how intuition saved them from catastrophe.

In October 1987, the UK was hit by a massive storm. Walking to work the next morning, I felt an increasing sense of unease. It was as if something extremely menacing was behind me, and the resulting anxiety caused me to pick up my pace. No sooner had I broken into a light jog than the gale-force winds detached a large branch from a tree and it crashed to the ground behind me. Had I not listened to my sense of unease and upped my pace, the branch would have landed on my head and I probably wouldn't have lived to tell the tale.

A few years later, I felt the same sense of unease while cycling home. Noticing that a car was slowing down as it approached the junction of a side road, I assumed the driver had seen me and was respecting my right of way. However, the sense of unease was so strong that I braked seconds before the driver pressed his foot on the accelerator and pulled out right in front of me. His car would have hit me had I not stopped at that moment.

That person may in future determine threat by the feeling they experienced at the moment of deciding to run:

experience = memory = association = intuition with precedent

Can you identify a time in your past when you have used intuition with precedent? Write in your journal and describe this time. It may not have been as dramatic as the example above; it could simply have been that you parked in a different parking space one evening, only to find the next morning that something had happened where you normally park. In defining your experience, paint a picture with your words. Use as much description as possible.

Intuition without precedent

Intuition without precedent happens without any warning or forethought. This type of intuition is always 100% true, and it can be developed and relied on. It is just like training your radar on what is happening in front of you. However, it takes time and commitment to allow yourself to do so.

Intuition without precedent is the sort of insight you have while you're busy doing other things. It comes unsought from the divine knowing of the universe. You could be washing up, and all of a sudden you will say to yourself, 'Someone is coming to visit' or 'I know now how to solve that problem'. Often these days, I will think about someone, only to have that someone knocking on my door the very same day.

In your journal, describe a time when intuition without precedent may have happened to you.

Intuition without precedent is the more powerful type of intuition to harness. I use mine all the time; it has saved me from making many mistakes and missing valuable opportunities. The key for this particular type of intuition is to have a focused and still mind.

EXERCISE 15

Here is a ten-minute exercise which will demand some focus. Find a quiet space, with no music, or television, or kids. Shut yourself in the bathroom if you have to. Sit quietly, get comfortable, close your eyes, and breathe. That is all I want you to do – just sit, relax and breathe, eyes closed, for ten minutes.

Notice what happens when you close your eyes and bring your attention to taking a deep breath. What is happening in your mind? Are there words, colours, thoughts? Can you hear songs?

I want you to watch your thoughts. See how they dart around, for example: 'Oh, I forgot to pay... I wonder what... I am tired... I have to call... I want that... I hated...' And so on and so forth. At the end of ten minutes, write down as many things as you can remember about your quiet time. How busy was your mind?

A person who uses intuition without precedent is different. They are able to still the chatter in their head and rest the mind for a few minutes at will. You can learn to do this, and I would encourage you to work on this concept of stillness regularly. The more you use this technique, the faster your stress will clear and your intuitive ability will flourish.

How intuition can work for you

We can all be intuitive. This is true regardless of our personality, culture, or religious background. We simply have to discover how intuition works for us to expand this ability.

Perhaps you had a hunch to strike up a conversation with another person, and looking back, you realise that conversation was the beginning of a close friendship. Possibly you had an image of yourself doing something in the future, and that exact vision came true in your life. Maybe you had the urge to travel another way home from work, only to find out later that there was a bad car crash on your usual route. All these events represent the workings of the intuitive faculty of your mind.

I am not discounting rationality. Rational decision making is important. However, we can complement our strategic thinking with our intuitive ability. When we apply intuitive thoughts, we can enhance our levels of success, fulfillment, and prosperity almost miraculously.

Following your intuition, you will find it easier to align with your journey and destination. Your self-worth and self-trust will skyrocket because you are listening to your thoughts, carefully choosing which ones have gravitas and which are simply noise. You can work with your conscious and unconscious mind to learn what your next steps should be. Intuition allows you to live in faith rather than fear.

Intuition can also alert you to something. Several years ago, my family home was burgled. That night, I put my son to bed, and instead of wishing him a good night and reminding him how much I loved him, I kept repeating to him that he was safe and I was there to protect him. I caught myself thinking that those words weren't the ones that I usually chose and questioning my thinking. Consciously, I was not aware that several hours later, a stranger would come into our home while we were sleeping to rummage through our belongings. Since that night, though, I have always paid attention to my intuition in my personal and professional life.

Some people feel intuition in their body – they get a gut feeling or bad vibes. If this is you, it may be a good starting point to pay attention to your body to tap into your intuition. Sometimes, intuition comes through an external sign – you see something over and over again. Others analyse their dreams. For them, dreams have a purpose and message that their unconscious mind is communicating back to them.

Ways to tune into your intuition:

Tune out distraction. Have a quiet time every day. Your intuition is subtle, and your conscious self is loud, so you need to quieten the mind, which quietens the conscious self. In the quiet, you can hear your intuition better.

Write down your intuitive hits. Acknowledge them to yourself. It honours and validates your intuition. When you see how often your intuitive hits are right on the money, it will help you trust it more when you make decisions.

Make a distinction. When you have a decision to make, tune into the voice of your intuition. Write down what the intuition is saying and what your conscious mind is saying. It will help you separate the two and feel and hear your intuition better.

Look at outside feedback. Intuition may come through external signs. You need to pay attention to these signs. They may be subtle or not so subtle.

Practise following your intuition on the little things, so that when the big things come along, you can trust it.

Have fun. When you have fun, it is easier to access your intuition. The answer you are struggling to find can pop into your head. Trust that the answer will present itself.

Tap into your intuition rather than asking for opinions and advice from other people. When you're asking for advice, you are not listening to your intuition. By trusting your intuition, you are showing you value it.

Living in the moment

How often have you driven to the supermarket without thinking about it? How many time have you eaten a meal and not savoured it? Days can pass by while our minds are elsewhere, yet life unfolds in the here and now.

Living in the moment – also called mindfulness – is a state of open, intentional attention on the present. When you become mindful, you realise that you are not your thoughts. You actually become an observer of your thoughts without judging them. Mindfulness involves being with your thoughts as they are, neither grasping them nor pushing them away.

There are many benefits to living in the moment. It can help reduce stress, lower blood pressure, and boost immune functioning. People who are living in the moment:

- Are happier, more exuberant, empathetic, and secure

- Can hear negative feedback without feeling threatened

- Fight less with their romantic partners

- Are more accommodating and less defensive

While it takes practice to live in the moment, throughout the years I've found the following advice helpful:

Loosen up. Giving a speech? Delivering a presentation? There is no need to think too hard about it or be perfect at it. This will just make you more anxious. Focusing on the present takes away your self-evaluation, allowing you to let go.

Savour the moment. When you're with your friends or family, are you still connected to your mobile phone? Shut it off completely and enjoy the conversation. Savour each moment, asking questions and finding out more about the people you care about.

Go with the flow. Do you find yourself having to control every aspect of your day? Take a holiday from it and allow yourself to go with the flow. When you go out with friends or your partner, if you usually pick the movie or the restaurant, allow them to make the choices.

Accept what is. We all have irritants in our lives. The mind's tendency if we can't avoid them is to focus on negative feelings, causing more stress. Sometimes, things are beyond our control, so embrace the feeling for what it is. It doesn't mean that you have to like what is happening or are resigned to it.

Pay attention. You become more mindful of the moment by paying attention to your immediate experience. Test it right now. What is happening in this instant? What can you see, hear, and smell? Observe the moment, but don't judge it or form an opinion.

When you find yourself distracted, anticipating what someone will say, or judging what they have just said, focus on your breathing to bring yourself back to the moment. Living in the moment is not a goal or a destination; you're already there. And something quite remarkable happens when you're in the moment. Often, the very thing you've been wishing for arrives because you are present to greet it.

Professional athletes are a good example of people who live in the moment. Once an athlete gets on the racing track, they tune out everything and immerse themselves in the race, rarely even acknowledging the presence of their competitors.

Living in the moment means giving your full attention to:

- The people you come into contact with on a daily basis – listen attentively

- The task that you are doing, such as driving, eating, writing, giving a speech, exercising, or relaxing

- Your actions and thoughts

In other words, living in the moment means letting go of any self-imposed pressure and huge expectations we have of ourselves. It helps us to take things easy, which in turn eases the nervousness that usually leads to low self-esteem.

Living in the moment does not mean we should not make plans for the future, we can simply avoid putting all our focus and energy on the past as that will steal our present and future. If someone has gone through a painful and traumatising past, they can choose to accept that past and the fact they cannot change it, and then move on more easily.

Be optimistic about the present and move towards the future with purpose. Our thoughts create our world and our actions are influenced by our outlook on life.

Here are some simple ways to live in the moment:

- Enjoy every moment you spend on any activity

- Practise gratitude on a daily basis

- Observe and enjoy your surroundings – do not overlook them

- Relax and feel peaceful

- Love your life

As I sit here and type, I realise that this is my life, right now. It won't begin when this book makes me money, or when I buy a large house, or take a trip round the world. Living in the moment is one of the most important skills to have when you're discovering yourself and true lasting happiness. It is an easy concept to grasp, and simultaneously difficult to get right. It takes hard work, practice and conscious awareness. With practice it can be achieved.

Every single person on this planet needs to allow themselves time to step back and reflect. It's essential for our well-being, especially in this hectic day and age. We don't have to have a fancy meditation room or sit Indian-style to do this; we can simply lie down or get comfortable in our favourite chair.

Close your eyes and just be. Be still. Be present. Let your mind empty. This is often referred to as meditation. While you're doing this, you can also practise some mindfulness techniques. Pay attention to how the soft fabric of the chair feels on your skin; listen to your breath; hear the birds chirping outside; taste and feel the water on your tongue while taking a drink. Life is made up of tiny sensations, feelings and moments. If you just wait for the big ones (e.g. getting a new car, getting married, taking a trip of a lifetime, getting a promotion), you will miss out on 90% of your life.

Have you ever arrived at work and not been able to remember anything about the journey there? If so, you were definitely not living in the moment. What did you miss? Did you miss beautiful clouds in the sky? A great song on the radio? Were you too busy repeating thousands of thoughts in your head?

Most of the time, our story – thoughts from yesterday or about tomorrow – makes us unable to live in the present. Our mind is always on the go, planning what we're going to say to this person, what we're going to wear to that event, or thinking about what he said, wondering if she liked our hair, analysing our co-worker's remark, etc. How can we take in the present with all that clutter going on?

We can simply decide to tune in to our life now. And that's exactly the reason we need to get some space, step back and reflect. Our lives are fragile and so precious. We can't plan on future events making us happy, that's like putting all our eggs in one basket. We don't even know if we will wake up tomorrow. We need to enjoy today, or else we are not really living.

To help you grasp the concept of living in the moment, here are some mindfulness techniques to get you started:

Be mindful for one minute. Set your stopwatch, sit comfortably, keep your eyes open and focus on your breath. Whenever a thought comes into your head, let it go and return to focusing on your breathing. This is a powerful exercise for building up your ability to be mindful. Don't beat yourself up if you struggle at first – this takes practice.

Conscious observation. Choose any object in your room – for example, a spoon, a shoe, or a pen – and just observe it. Pick it up and feel it. Really look at it as if it is the first time you've ever seen it. Don't assess it or judge it, and don't think about anything else while you are doing this.

Conscious doing. Do a simple task such as making a cup of tea, washing a dish, or brushing your teeth. Through every step of the task, really notice each sensation, focusing only on the task.

For example, if you're making a cup of tea, focus on choosing a mug. Feel the mug and look at it using conscious observation. When you get the tea out of the cupboard, notice how opening the cupboard feels. Smell the tea and focus on its scent. Now turn the tap on and run water, listening to the sounds it makes, feeling the water on your fingers. Fill the kettle with water and turn on the stove. Again, listen to the sounds, etc.

You see where this is going? Practise this for a simple task each day. You will get better and better at observing the present moment in your daily life. Remember, practice makes perfect.

These techniques are just a few ways to strengthen your ability to live consciously in each moment. Overall, it's important to remember that each day is a gift. Decide to be present and grateful that you have today without ruining it by reliving yesterday or wishing for tomorrow.

The power of the moment

Your true and real power to create, to grow, to build relationships exists in the present moment. When you are totally and completely focused on the moment, all of your energy is focused as well. Your mind is clear and laser sharp. Your emotions are centred and not scattered. You are prepared and energised to take action on whatever it is you want.

When you are in the present moment, your decision making becomes more in line with your purpose and direction. You become a better listener; you learn to listen with compassion and understanding, which leads to stronger relationships, both personally and professionally. You also learn to become a better listener to your own intuitive voice. Your mind quietens down, which allows the wisdom of your inner messages to seep through.

So begin today. Practise the skill of being present. When you consistently take action with clearly planned, focused intent in the direction of your goals and dreams, success is inevitable.

Create strategies to help you truly enjoy relationships with others. In my home, our mobile phone ban between the hours of 6.30 and 8.30pm allows us to connect with one another. Be a family. We now enjoy deep and meaningful evenings around the dinner table.

Here is an exercise which you may find useful to practise on a daily basis.

EXERCISE 16

This guided imagination exercise is called the body scan and is a way to induce self-hypnosis. You will need at least ten to fifteen minutes without interruptions.

You may find it helpful to read the following a few times to get used to it, and then read it into an audio recorder to play back as you stay in a relaxed position. (Important: do not drive while listening to any recorded exercises.) However, you can still learn to reach a relaxed trance state if you choose to participate while reading the book.

To begin, get as comfortable as you can in your chair with both feet flat on the ground. Take a moment to close your eyes and make sure you are comfortable. Then mentally scan your body from the inside. Start with the top of your head, through your forehead and neck, progressing slowly all the way down within body at your own pace. Visit each part of the body, to the soles of your feet. As you bring awareness into every area of your body, notice any areas that are holding stressor tension.

Pause.

Recognise these spots, and then move on, continuing to scan your body slowly. Become curious about what your body feels like.

Pause.

Allow yourself to take some relaxed, open belly breaths, letting the air fill your lungs. Feel the rise and fall of your belly.

Now imagine that your breath is going into one of the tense areas. Notice the area begin to loosen and relax as the breath goes in. Loosening. Relaxing. Again, breathe gently into that area, feeling relaxed. Breathe gently, loosening and relaxing; loosening and relaxing even more.

You may now choose to breathe into another part of the body. Feel that area begin to loosen and relax.

Pause.

Take a moment to notice the thoughts in your head. Just notice what's there right now; you don't have to do anything with them or to them. What are you thinking about right now? Do you see the thoughts floating in front of your mind's eye? Where do you sense the thoughts? Where do they reside in your body? Breathe gently and notice.

Pause.

Let the thoughts turn into clouds, floating in the blue sky of your mind's eye. Watch them float by you for a moment. Notice each thought in your mind transform easily and let it float by.

Pause.

Let the thought clouds go with each breath. Feel like a neutral observer, unattached, watching the clouds disappear over the horizon, getting smaller with each moment. The blue sky becomes clearer and clearer. The clouds are floating away, disappearing. You're breathing gently.

Pause.

Imagine that the blue sky has become you, become your whole body. Notice your body from your head down to your toes. As you inhale, allow the calming, radiant blue sky to fill your whole body and mind for a moment. You're completely clear, completely calm, completely at ease in the clarity. Enlarge the blue sky and let it fill you even more, relaxing into your breathing.

Pause.

Notice that the calmness and clarity naturally helps you to access any tools, any information you need for your daily life. As you take another gentle breath, become calmer, more relaxed, more at ease.

Pause.

When you are ready, open your eyes, bring yourself back into the room, stretch. Notice how you feel. Are you more relaxed, yet recharged?

Practise this exercise at least twice this week. Note down any changes in your work life.

Learning from the body

Being fully present, communicating mutually with others, and embodying our personal commitments to ourselves in service to the world – these are goals that are more easily accomplished through the alignment of our minds, hearts, and bodies.

When we view the world through our personality or ego, we live a life divided between how we believe we should be and the rules we have learned for behaving. This often leads to a gnawing feeling that we are either not acting in accordance with our true nature or are disconnected from a part of ourselves. Over time, as our recognition of this dissonance becomes more apparent, we ask ourselves why we don't feel satisfied and what our purpose is in life.

If we seek to regain access to our uniqueness through a greater understanding of our personality or ego, we are trying to solve problems using the same paradigm that created them. Engaging the wisdom of the body in our search provides clarity and a fuller understanding of our connection with and place in the world. The more we are able to connect with our uniqueness, the better we are at expressing that which we hold dear through our words and actions. The more we express our passion and motivation, the more impact we have on our lives.

Utilising what I call the Growth Spiral Process (GSP), we can learn to be in touch with and understand our connection to ourselves, our purpose, and others. The GSP is within us, and between us and others. Through our interactions and experiences, it changes our essence and that of the people we come into contact with.

The growth spiral is a never-ending process that includes:

- Awareness

- Centring

- Flow

- Purpose

Awareness

EXERCISE 17

Focus on your breath. Let yourself breathe naturally, following the breath as you inhale and exhale. Relax your abdominal muscles and allow your stomach to blow up like a balloon. Let the in breath fill your chest cavity, then when it feels appropriate, release the breath while making a vocal sound. Follow the breath until you have fully exhaled and it is time to take another breath, and repeat the cycle.

When you're exhaling, imagine the breath travelling to a spot either about 3 inches below your navel (your centre) or down through your feet into the ground. Body scan. Notice the places in your body where you tense in response to stress. Throughout the day, especially during difficult situations, scan your body. When you find tension, send a breath there. Remember to check your shoulders, chest, hands, face and jaw. Let go. Feel the back of your legs, buttocks and back against the surface and the weight of your body sinking deeper into your seat. Allow yourself to feel the sensation of gravity in your arms, legs, face and head.

EXERCISE 18

Sit or lie comfortably. Close your eyes and take three deep breaths in through your nose, exhaling through your mouth. Focus on your breathing, noticing your breath as you inhale and then exhale. Just notice what is without changing anything – the rising and falling of your chest and/or your abdomen as you breathe in. Feel the breath as it enters your body through your nose. If you notice any places in your body that are tense, send a breath there and release the tension, then return to your breathing. If you notice thoughts arising, gently return your attention to your breath. The idea is not to be without thoughts, but rather to notice when you have them and return your focus to your breathing.

Continue for ten to twenty minutes.

Centring

EXERCISE 19

A simple strategy for centring yourself is to place both feet on the floor and feel your groundedness.

Doing this during difficult situations brings you into the present and provides a solid foundation for your responses.

Stand with your arms at your sides, relaxed. Place your feet approximately shoulder width apart, finding a distance that is comfortable. Bend your knees slightly while straightening your back, and feel your body lifting as if a thread was pulling you upward. Allow your head to tilt downward slightly, releasing the stress in your neck.

You may do this exercise with your eyes open or closed. If you do it with your eyes open, allow your gaze to focus slightly downward a few feet in front of you. Feel the bottoms of your feet touching the ground. Rock backwards and forwards and side-to-side, ending in a comfortable grounded position. As you stand there, scan your body and release any tension you feel. Take two or three deep breaths, making a sound as you exhale. Focus your attention on the sound until the breath is fully exhaled, and allow your natural rhythm to lead into the next breath.

Now, focus on gravity. See if you can feel the effect of gravity on your arms, legs, face, and head. Allow your face muscles to relax and your jaw to drop.

Study the energy field around you. Can you sense the same amount of space in front of you as to the back, right and left, above your head and below your feet? Spend a few seconds in each space, sensing and imagining the space around you. Lastly, feel the sense of gravity throughout your body.

When you go into difficult situations centred, you are more available and more present. Doing this exercise fully can take a couple of minutes, but you can do briefer versions throughout the day. Whenever you notice yourself tensing, allow yourself to move back into centre. It will become second nature after a while, and you will feel centred even when you're not practising.

Flow

Two or three times each day, reflect on conversations or experiences that you've had when you were fully present and experiencing flow. Journal about these experiences – how they made you feel and what the results were. Then reflect upon times when you were not fully engaged in the experiences you were having. Journal about these experiences – how they made you feel and what the results were.

Once a week, review your journal and make a commitment to creating opportunities to experience flow. For example, before entering into a conversation, take a walk with your dog, find time to get out into nature, or simply engage in the centring or body scan exercises. Focus your attention on being present, bring yourself back when you notice that you are drifting away, and experience flow in this new way.

After completing these activities, journal about what they were like for you.

Purpose

Often when we're trying to reason through problems, the right answer is the one that 'feels' right. Living and learning is not just about concepts and ideas, but also the experiences of our body and the process of being alive. Living more fully in our body, we incorporate a sense of purpose. Once we've identified our purpose and put it into words, we express our passion, motivation, and commitment to the future from the centre of our being. Our words become actions, and when they are connected with our aliveness or excitement, we embody our intentions. This paves the way for creating what matters most to us in the world. What was simply a feeling or thought becomes a reality.

Answering the following questions may help you to identify what matters to you:

- What is important to me?

- For what purpose is it important to me?

- Who is important to me?

- Why are they important to me?

- How do I want to live my life?

- What is a satisfying and fufilling life?

These questions deepen our understanding of our purpose. When we communicate the answers from a centred state, our purpose takes on a power that comes from the alignment of our heart, mind and body.

For example, my personal purpose statement is to be fully present and connect compassionately. While this intention satisfies my need to feel at peace and give to others, it also allows others to feel touched by our interactions and be motivated themselves to make the world a more peaceful place. This same purpose supports all of my practices, be it running, sitting, or centring. They are all part of my bigger intention to be a model for peace in the world.

The process of awareness, centre, flow, and purpose is never ending as we continue to change and be changed by the world. As we work with our personal stories, we will return to awareness. When we declare our commitment to our purpose, we feel centred and connected to the commitment.

The skills associated with the growth spiral process are easily learned, but they require commitment to practise being more present and connected to the world. We become whatever we do repeatedly. The congruence of these skills is powerful, but we must embark on this journey of self-exploration gently.

EXERCISE 20

Begin with basic meditation, then write down the truest statement about yourself right now. Sit with the statement and notice what thoughts or feelings come and go. Is there a statement you could write that would be truer than the one you've written? If so, what is it? Write it down. If not, stay with what you've already written.

Repeat the process with any new thoughts that come and go, then simply sit with the truth about yourself in this moment. Bring your attention back to your breath, and sit with the statements that come and any feelings they raise.

EXERCISE 21

Again beginning with basic meditation, ask yourself the following questions:

What if it really doesn't matter what you do? What if all that matters is how you do it? What would you do then? How would you do it?

Let thoughts or feelings come and go, and sit with them. When you're ready, write down any of the thoughts you'd like to reflect on later. Bring your attention back to your breathing. Just be with your breathing for a few moments, then ask yourself, 'What would I do if it weren't so risky?'

Again, write down your responses then return to your breathing for a few moments.

When you're ready, complete the following statement:

My purpose is to… in a way that… so that… happens.

Continue to write complete statements without judging what you are writing or needing the statements to be perfect. Just go with whatever comes.

When you can no longer come up with new statements, put your pen down and spend a few minutes with what you've written. You may want to come back to this exercise a number of times during the week as you work on what arises within you.

Review your notes and reflections from these two exercises to see what has the most meaning for you and feels like your personal truth. Then work on a statement that underscores your commitment to yourself and the world. Your statement should naturally evolve into a simple one that suggests what is most important to you, and that will be the foundation for the choices you make in your life. Be patient and listen to what arises from within you.

To conclude our work for this week, reflect on your last six weeks and listen to the emotions in your gut. Follow the body scan experience – what has come up? Is there anything missing? Are you grateful for what you have achieved so far? Write everything down.

Trust in the present, be kind to your past, and engage with yourself fully and deeply as you learn to work alongside your intuition.

Week Seven

It All Ends With Your Beginning

Once you move towards being committed, you attract others who are committed. If you're growing, you attract other people who are growing, which puts you in a position to start creating a network of like-minded individuals. Help each other to succeed. Visualise your desired outcomes at all times, involving yourself in personal development to feel a sense of accomplishment in every area of your life. It feels great to live on the win/win side of the equation.

You have learned how to understand your own emotions to succeed, learned more about your conscious and unconscious behaviours, learned to take time to listen to your thoughts, and learned to take your life forward in the direction you feel is right for you. Have you noticed a glint in your eye; a skip in your step; a positive change in your life that you wished to make just a few weeks ago? Notice the key changes you have made for yourself. They may be small from the outsitde, but inside, something new is roaring. Maybe you have achieved your goal, or maybe you still have some way to go.

This week we will be focusing on where to go from here to ensure your positive change is set for the long term. Positive change deserves all your effort and attention.

You are a unique human being and have a unique way of moving forward. Your way. What I will now ask you to do is to think of one word, one powerful word that epitomises your whole experience. This may take you a little while, and that is a good thing as it will help you take a step back, examine all your learnings and integrate them into who you are today.

When you have your powerful word, write it in your journal. Sometimes, you may find yourself struggling to calm yourself and bring down your energy level so that you can experience deep stillness. More often than not, your powerful word will help you find your way back to the core of who you are. Use it like a mantra.

You are unique

Check the palms of your hands. Then take a close look at your family members' and friends' palms. Compare them. What is your observation?

You are absolutely unique. Each line on your palm traces your individuality, your own path. No one else can dictate in which direction you will go. You carry a unique package the world is waiting to appreciate.

I think that everyone on this planet has their own place, their own purpose. They help the world to evolve and grow. The more humanity seems to degrade itself, the more everyone can find their place and achieve their full potential. No-one else can present you better than you can. You and you alone show the world the best of who you are.

Your biggest and final obstacle as you move forward is your ego. Now, the ego is not a bad thing. On the contrary. It is, however, little understood.

The ego is constructed of many things which build the story of ourselves, and a fascinating story it is, too. It creates and maintains what we would describe as our identity. Our ego starts with our parents' beliefs, and potentially with their parents' beliefs beforehand. Where we come from holds a significant clue as to how we will have created our ego.

Then, the story continues with our schooling and our culture. What language we speak; what media we have have access to; the social groups we have created around us.

I often compare the ego to a shopping trolley. For example, if I buy a posh car, I will put it in my shopping trolley and parade it around. I have worked hard for this car, and in a way it demonstrates my perceived success.

The issue to be aware of is that our ego is deeply engrained within us. To use the shopping trolley metaphor again, once I have put my flash car into my trolley, I may start fearing its disappearance. What if circumstances in life require me to lose the car? Who am I then? As it represents success to me, would I then be a failure?

And then fear creeps in. Fear being one of the most daunting emotions to work on, this is where many of us get stuck.

A friend of mine, Marie, had been married for over ten years when her husband, Ralph, suddenly started resenting her for his failures. If he was hurting, surely she had to suffer too? He blamed her for his unhappiness, making sure she knew who the boss was.

Ralph's controlling patterns were obvious to me every time I visited Marie. Marie was clearly unhappy and aware of the damage this situation was causing to herself and her two beautiful sons. Somehow, though, she couldn't bear to leave. Her ego was urging her to stay in the life that she had always known, as if the walls of her unhappy home would keep her safe.

Finally, Marie did find the courage to rebuild her life, and oh boy, what a trip of self-discovery she's had. Although at one time she hit rock bottom in terms of self-esteem and self-love, she is now stronger than I have ever seen her. Her boys have also learned a significant lesson in terms of self-respect and pride.

After several years of learning Tai Chi, I was recently put back into the beginners' group having missed about ten months of classes due to the birth of my daughter. I was horrified and took the news as a slap in the face, but I continued to practise. Applying myself to the instructions

I was given, I found a new way of moving my body. Going back to square one had given me the opportunity to fine tune my flow as I uncovered a new depth and understanding. It was simply my ego that had been bruised by being put back into the beginners' class. I had to give my ego space to acknowledge what had happened, and then move on.

Ultimately, we are the ones driving our shopping trolleys. The trolley never drives us. We can choose to take our ego for what it is and go in our own direction, taking a risk to serve who we truly are.

EXERCISE 22

Reflect on the components of your ego and what they mean to you. Why are some elements dear to you? Are they truly important to you? Are they how you want to live your life, or do they simply tell your story?

Write down the components of your ego related to:

- Your upbringing

- What your parents/siblings/family taught you

- Significant items in your life

- Additional items in your ego shopping trolley

Now underline each component you see as purposeful in your life – those that bring you joy, carry you forward and sound true to who you are. Take some time to reflect on this, then ask yourself, 'Who am I?'

Write your answer down, then answer the question again using different words.

Write your answer down, then answer the question one final time, again using different words.

You cannot be like others. Accept this fact and mould yourself the way you are. This will create self-respect and develop self-esteem.

It's interesting to note that if everybody praises you, you will naturally develop self-esteem, self-confidence and pride. If you choose to accept criticism, it will also impact your self-esteem. You will develop enthusiasm and enhance your energy to perform better. I will argue that you have to receive praise *and* criticism to protect your self-esteem, self-respect, develop your personality, and progress to achieve success. However, some people tend to become crushed by criticism.

If you are losing your self-esteem due to the influence of your environment, understanding the following will help to overcome the problem.

Everybody in this world is imperfect. This is what makes us perfect. Identify and accept your strengths and weaknesses. It is your journey that made you who you are today. You have the power to go in whichever direction you choose for yourself

Do not compare yourself with others. There is no need to compare your shopping trolley with anyone else's. You are unique and your path is your own.

Identify and shed your negative attitudes. A woman I work with told me last week how she struggled with her weight. She was being careful right now, but knew deep inside that she would fail to lose weight. She had such a negative attitude that she was guaranteed to fail – until she chose to embrace the positive potential of living a healthy lifestyle.

Recognise any negative patterns in yourself.

Lack of self-esteem leads to self-pity. Self-pity kills your confidence. It is a vicious circle. A positive attitude will go a significant way to helping you break old habits. Aim to find the positive in everything, consciously.

Keep away from people who bring you down. Also, refrain from bringing other people down.

It is easy when we are hurting to hurt others too. I used to have a circle of friends I now call the 'me too club'. When one of us had issues with a partner, someone else would be miserable and join in. When one of us had a bad boss, another would too. We kept each other company in this negative spiral – life was terrible, but we were all in it together.

It is fine to maintain friendships, but be conscious of what they bring to your life.

Do not look down on anyone. In any society, some people look down on others. This is foolish. Do not attach importance to the physical appearance, colour, intelligence, social standing, sexuality, etc. of others. Everyone is unique and beautiful in their own way.

Recognise that your uniqueness is empowering. Only your specific strengths, talents, abilities, and skills will be able to keep you moving forward. You can certainly learn new skills and discover new abilities, but it's still you who is responsible for making positive changes to achieve your goals.

Let's go back to your one powerful word. Associate all the good memories of the results you have achieved and the positive changes you have noticed over the past six weeks with this one word. Seal it all in. This is your gift to yourself. You may need to sit and ponder on your word from time to time, reminding yourself that you are worth all the effort. Being kind and trusting yourself will get you far further than beating yourself up.

While writing this book, I set myself my own goal – to evolve and push further towards my purpose of being a catalyst for change, all while taking better care of my body and soul – one that will not be achieved in seven weeks, but will be even more life-changing. I am treating this final chapter as the beginning of a new adventure, looking at it with excitement and wonder. This process has been educational for me and something within me has changed.

And change is exactly what I want us to think about in the next section.

Change – the only constant

In our lives, we come across so much change. Change is a necessary part of life. It is through change that we grow, adapt, and work out problems as they arise.

To manage change effectively and be prepared for it, we must anticipate what is coming next. If we're caught by surprise, we are in danger of becoming overwhelmed.

The parable of the boiled frog helps us to understand the nature of change. If you place a frog into a pot of boiling water, it will leap out of the pan when it feels the heat. However, if you place the frog in a pan of cold water, without sensing any danger, the frog will stay. When you place the pan on the stove and slowly heat the water, the frog relaxes. The heating water drains away the frog's energy. By the time the frog realises the danger, it is too late to take action.

Please note: no frog was harmed in the process of writing this book.

When change happens gradually, it goes unnoticed. To avoid becoming a boiled frog, we need to be vigilant and not let unexpected changes creep up on us. In today's fast changing world, we have neither the time nor the energy to react to change. We must be prepared by being proactive. If we know far enough in advance what is on the horizon, we can make plans and perhaps even transform the change into an opportunity.

Making any positive change in our lives can be a big decision, as well as the start of a long journey. It is easy to have a dream about where we want to be, who we want to be, or how we want to be, but often we underestimate the amount of effort it will take to get there. This can make us stop our dreams and ambitions in their tracks, or worse, never start the journey at all.

It doesn't matter how big or small the goal you want to achieve is; what matters is that you take a positive step to start the ball rolling.

> *'A journey of a thousand miles*
> *begins with a single step.'*
>
> ———————
>
> **LAO TZU**

Life can flow harmoniously if you welcome change with open arms. Problems are inevitable. You cannot run from them, hide from them, or avoid them.

I like to think of our lives as being like a stream, and the problems we encounter are rocks. As long as we continue flowing, we can flow past the rocks. If the flow becomes strong enough, the rocks may get dislodged. It is not how many problems we have which determines our quality of life, but rather how we have learned to deal with them.

Change the way you think about change so that you see it as an opportunity instead of a setback. Learn to work with your emotions. Understand your emotions and listen to them. For example, allow yourself to cry if you feel hurt. Emotions can provide you with feedback about what is going on inside you. Are the emotions you're feeling well founded or just a reflection of your surroundings? Are they linked to an event in the past? Are they keeping you safe/stuck? Are they telling you not to go somewhere?

One good way to learn to adapt to change is by making changes in your life. Start with something small like a new hairstyle, exercise plan or diet. Or you could change one of your rituals. Instead of turning on the TV when you get home, pick up the phone and call a friend or hop on the treadmill. Make a commitment to yourself and journal your progress. At the end of the first week, notice the difference in yourself and your attitude to change.

I used to work with Tanya. Tanya was an incredible asset to our HR team and one of the friendliest people I knew, but change distressed her. She would cry at the slightest whiff of change.

Instead of preventing herself from feeling fear, she simply learned to accept the feelings for what they were rather than what she thought they represented. Acceptance is big when we look at fear. It's OK to feel whatever you are feeling; it's what you do with it that matters.

Journey like water

Water cannot be contained. Sooner or later, it escapes and embarks on its own journey. A river follows the contours of the land; the easiest route; the path of least resistance. If the landscape changes, the river changes course and eventually finds its journey's end: the sea.

To be successful, your journey of self-improvement must be like that of a river. Along the way, it will take many turns. You'll encounter what seem to be insurmountable obstacles, but like water, you'll find a way to flow around them. At times, the river will disappear deep underground. You'll lose sight of it, but it must resurface eventually, as all rivers do to reach journey's end.

Your journey will not always be smooth. You'll encounter rapids and waterfalls, and may have to take enormous leaps of faith, and when you reach the next step along the journey, your power and energy will have increased massively. You will also experience stagnant pools, and continue to flow with the river and it will eventually flow freely and cleanly again.

Don't try to contain your river of self-development. Let the river find its own route. A river moves, changes, adapts and grows bigger. All rivers eventually flow out to the sea. They all reach journey's end, and you will too.

I love this analogy so much. Water naturally flows to the lowest level. Whether it is draining down the gutters in the street or tumbling down a majestic waterfall, it flows down. According to Taoism, we as humans can learn humility from the way water naturally flows.

When we boast of an accomplishment, we are putting ourselves above others. To elevate ourselves in this way is not natural. If we were like water, we would keep moving forward rather than making a big production out of certain events in out lives.

Water is also patient. Over time, it can wear out the densest material. The tides create new shorelines every moment, and water flowing over riverbeds carves out the hardest of stone. Where we may give up when circumstances appear to be hopeless, water carries on.

Water is emotional and moody, which bears a striking resemblance to our human emotions. Try to contain us for too long and we'll desire freedom, releasing ourselves to flow.

Water is flexible. It freezes in the winter, thaws in the spring, and rises and falls in the form of precipitation. Water remains; only its form changes. If we used this natural ability to move with nature, we would become more tuned in to how to be, rather than what to do.

Going with the flow of life

We get to choose what kind of day we're going to have. Are we going to let life's events control us? Will we let them pull us down into our own self-created hell, or will we take a stand within ourselves and say no?

We simply have to believe in the changes that will lead to the happiness we seek. A doorway leads to a hallway with even more doors, more choices, more decisions if we trust ourselves to make the right choices and recognise the opportunities as they present themselves. Like water, we flow in and out of these doors, moving around obstacles. No matter what, the experience we gain will be beneficial to our growth or it wouldn't have been presented to us in the first place. There are no mistakes.

The universe has a natural flow. Not only are we influenced by the universe's natural flow, we also need to be aligned with it, emotionally, energetically and spiritually. When we are in disharmony, we experience mishaps, disruptions and suffering.

The universal laws are interrelated and founded on the understanding that everything is energy. There are twelve universal laws and twenty-one sub-laws – guidelines to assist us to be in alignment with the universe's natural flow. Going with the flow means being non-resistant to the natural flow of life, activities and doings.

Water is the epitome of non-resistance. The Grand Canyon is arguably the grandest example of water expressing its natural flow. During floods, water sweeps everything before it in a torrential outburst. Little can withstand its force.

> *'It doesn't matter where you are coming from. All that matters is where you are going.'*
>
> ————————
>
> **BRIAN TRACY**

As human beings, we are programmed to want more, and this is what has contributed to our evolution. So now is the time to get up (metaphorically) and look at everything you have achieved so far. Think of ten key life achievements and the pivotal moments that led to them, then write them down in your journal.

Take a moment and reflect on the past seven weeks. Where exactly are you seven weeks on? How have your progressed alongside your goals? Do you have more of an inkling what your destination may be? Are you any closer to achieving your dreams now? Think about all that you have achieved over the last seven weeks and what the pivotal moments have been for you. Where were you? What did you achieve? Have you achieved all of your goals and milestones? If not, what is left for you to do? How do you know when you will have achieved it all?

Write all your answers in your journal.

Achieving your goals

What's the secret? It's so simple. Invest in yourself. You've invested the last seven weeks' work, effort and energy into yourself. In fact, you have invested years into you in different ways, so what about the future? Will you give it your all?

Once you start investing in you, success will come automatically. You can choose to live a healthier and happier life by putting in place simple strategies. Here are my top five:

- Plan the week ahead

- Constantly seek to learn new things

- Limit screen time and fake social interaction

- Nurture the relationships that matter to me

- Play

What are yours?

If meditation isn't your thing, I'd recommend you take five minutes out of each day to visualise and immerse yourself in your ideal situation. Experience your dreams as if they were real. Focus on what you want and let go of what you don't want. What you do not want doesn't matter.

My precious little boy is four. Bless his heart, most of the time, if he does not want to do something, he will start to cry. The other day it was something as trivial as not wanting to eat a banana, and the big tears were rolling down his cheaks. I explained to him that it doesn't matter what he doesn't want, he can tell me what he wants instead. If he would rather not go to school today, we focus on the good times he will have with his friends at playtime, or how proud his teacher will be with his hard work and dedication.

It is as simple as this for us, too. It is difficult to make something that we do not want shift; it is a lot easier to get what we want instead. Imagine yourself driving towards your destination – your dream – and your car breaks down. You're exactly halfway there, so do you walk towards your dream or back home?

What does it take to be a successful person?

Successful achievers are flexible and adaptable as well as being incurably postive. They have not one dream, but many. Any dream or goal requires plans. And plans require conscious work.

Successful people work hard. They do what it takes to make their dreams come true. When you work at doing something, the end result is always more enjoyable.

They don't take no for an answer. Nobody has the right to stop you from achieving your dreams. Ralph was unable to keep Marie down. When she rose up and left her unhappy marriage, she quite literally shone.

They focus. By concentrating on your goals and objectives, you will find that you achieve more. You won't get sidetracked or procrastinate. By focusing, you will be able to do things effectively and be highly productive.

They take action. If you don't know how to do what you need for success, learn, or ask for help. I surround myself with like-minded individuals and enjoy being part of a community of mutual help and support. Expanding your knowledge base is essential for achievement. When you know how to do something, move on to the next thing. Never waste time; you are only delaying your enjoyment of your dream if you do.

They don't make excuses. Successful people make decisions. When you make a decision, follow it. If it doesn't work out, learn from it. Don't put decisions off for fear of making a wrong one.

They learn from their mistakes. There is no failure, only feedback. Mistakes are something to learn from. If you make a mistake, correct it, then move on. Let go of guilt – you did what you could with the resources available at the time of your mistake.

They are passionate. When you are passionate about something, you will find that people respond positively. Opportunities will be presented to you and you will be ready to receive them. Who would you rather be around – someone who is excited or someone who is bored?

They are personable. Be friendly. Learn how to lead and influence people. Everybody needs help to succeed, and if you're a nice person, others will be far more likely to offer their help and support. Nobody will want to see you fail.

Help others, and they will help you.

They reward themselves. My favourite part! Take a deep breath and revisit all of your positive actions of the last seven weeks. Now is the time to reap the rewards. Name three things that you think you deserve to do for having worked so hard on yourself, and three further things to reward yourself with when you have achieved your own personal goal

In conclusion

Change, dreams, intentions must be about you. Intentions that depend on someone else are not likely to work. Your change may ultimately benefit others, but it won't be about your inner desire to change for yourself. Use your intuition to guide you to the change or dream that really speaks to you and moves your soul. It is never selfish to take time to build a life you desire from the soul outward.

Keep your focus. Now you are completing the steps towards your dream, you must keep up your focus and positivity. Imagine the end results on a regular basis. Imagine how you will feel living with your achievement. Constantly link things in your daily life to your current step, and to the end goal or achievement. This will help imprint the positives in your brain, and as your brain cannot tell the difference between an imagined act and an actual act, it will believe you have already achieved it. Then achieving it again will be simple.

Keep taking those steps. Often the first step is the biggest hurdle. Achieving anything you want is a process of steps, so keep the process rolling. Constantly navigate towards the end goal and achievement.

If you are the sort of person who gets disheartened easily, don't keep looking at all the steps you have yet to achieve. Look at what you need to do to complete the step you are on, along with how many steps you have covered. However many steps you need to achieve your goal, you are already on your way.

Stay flexible/adaptable. Life will challenge you and provide you with many opportunities to turn back, give up, and doubt yourself. Find some type of mechanism or spiritual tool, like a prayer, symbol, affirmation, or practice (e.g. yoga, meditation, going out into nature), that snaps you back into the reality of universal flow.

Do not resist. As challenges come up, do not fight them. Simply listen to what they are saying and allow them to pass through. Challenges and setbacks can be highly instructional and helpful. If they seem to be trying to persuade you to give up, become aware of the ruse and re-centre yourself to your intention. Contemplate and identify what part of you was most compromised by the challenge and look for a way to break down that barrier.

Don't grade yourself. If you stray off your path, do not fret. Forward progress can never be removed. And one of the most amazing gifts we have been given is that each moment is new. It may seem like you have been set back, but the work you have done towards your intention will still have been done, waiting to be picked up where you left off. Begin again. And if you slip, begin once more.

Reward yourself along the way. This is important. By taking time to reward yourself for each achievement, you build your excitement. It also means you are enjoying the journey. This way you cannot fail.

Visualise. Use the Law of Attraction. Imagine how you will feel once you have achieved the end result. Live it. Act as if you have already achieved it – dress the part and act the part.

Resources are never a barrier. You have already been gifted with the most amazing resource you will ever need, and that is you. Set your intention, begin your journey, and the resources you need will come.

Your life is now. Everyone puts things off for another day. But our procrastination sets us up for guilt, frustration, and discouragement. The next thing we know, we are out of school, or our kids have grown, or we've lost someone, or we have moved on to a new relationship, house, or job, without doing the many things we promised ourselves we would do.

Please do not let life pass you by. Live from a deeper purpose and squeeze the juice out of every single day.

Pursuing a life with purpose and meaning is not only good from a spiritual point of view, it is also common sense. If we do not do something to change our lives, no one else will. By doing nothing, we are choosing to allow the chaos and uncertainty of each hour to consume us. This is not living; this is merely existing.

We started this process by setting your goals. Once the goals have been set, let them go. It's like programming your GPS. Set the address of where you want to go, then just drive and trust the GPS to take you there. Roadblocks or traffic may challenge your progress, but keep on moving towards your destination. Take time occasionally to reconnect with both your vision and its purpose. Do not give up.

Remember to be grateful. Keep joy in your heart. Positive thinking creates positive energy. Fun makes everything more worthwhile.

We all make mistakes. Now is the time for you to truly be you. Learn from everything, stay aware of who you are, what your purpose is and what you stand for, and you can't go wrong.

As you move on to the next chapter of your life, I am going to ask you three things:

- What are you most proud of having achieved in these seven weeks?

- What are your leanings?

- Where are you going from here?

Once you have answered these three reflective questions, please consider sending your answers to me at the email address below. Not only would I love to build from your learnings in the next chapter of my own life, but I would also like to share some of your successes online in my 'Success story of the month'. Tell me what you have achieved and how you got there. My aim is to create a list of practical tips and stories to share with other members of my community.

You can also send your email address to: hello@verytraining.co.uk

or join the VeryT page on Facebook: www.facebook.com/verytraining/

I would be delighted to add you to my newsletter mailing list for up-to-date success stories, blogs, resources and offers on forthcoming training programmes. (I promise none of your information will be sold, rented or sent to third parties.)

It has been my pleasure, honour and joy to accompany you on your journey. Do keep in touch, and I hope that our paths will cross in the near future.

And with that, over and out – Julie.

ACKNOWLEDGEMENTS

I am lucky to have too many amazing people out there to acknowledge – friends, colleagues, teachers, trainers, mentors. I am deeply grateful for all of my life's events, which have led me to this particular moment.

I'd like to thank my amazing team at VeryHR, VeryT and Rethink Press specifically for dealing with my moments of complete unstructured madness and for their ongoing words of encouragement. Thank you for dealing with me each and every day!

My life has been shaped by you, and as you read these words, I personally am looking forward to our next chapters together. Thank you for being my teachers. Always remember, you are never alone.

ABOUT THE AUTHOR

Julie Provino's passion lies in providing tangible results and being in the business of changing lives for the better, whether she is spearheading the Provino household, managing the growth of boutique international HR services company VeryHR Ltd, coaching and mentoring individuals, or delivering training through VeryT to companies and the general public. She strongly believes that how we see ourselves at work and in our private lives is undergoing a complete transformation, and that a world of new opportunities is arising, with collective awareness as the way forward.

For additional help and support in achieving your 'seven weeks to get what you want' journey, why not attend one of VeryT's workshops of the same name (see www.verytraining.co.uk) or purchase the accompanying workbook.

Julie and her team also offer additional training in certified NLP, mindfulness, leadership, team effectiveness, additional bespoke programmes, and individual coaching and support.

You can contact Julie via www.veryhr.co.uk,
www.verytraining.co.uk or
by email at hello@verytraining.co.uk.